# A GREATER FREEDOM

*Stories of Faith from Operation Iraqi Freedom*

# A GREATER FREEDOM

*Stories of Faith from Operation Iraqi Freedom*

# OLIVER NORTH
### EXECUTIVE EDITOR
### STORIES BY SARA HORN

**BROADMAN & HOLMAN PUBLISHERS**

Nashville, Tennessee

© 2004 by Broadman & Holman Publishers
All rights reserved
Printed in the United States of America

0-8054-3153-5

Published by Broadman & Holman Publishers,
Nashville, Tennessee

Dewey Decimal Classification: 956.7044
Subject Heading: IRAQ WAR, 2003—PICTORIAL WORKS \ FREEDOM

All interior photographs by Jim Veneman unless otherwise specified.
Photograph on page 110 reprinted with permission of *The News and Observer*, Raleigh, N.C.
Cover photograph by Arko Datta.
Content from *USS Truman*, courtesy Baptist Press.
Page design by Diana Lawrence. Editing by Lawrence Kimbrough.

All Scripture quotations, unless otherwise indicated,
are taken from the Holman Christian Standard Bible®
Copyright © 1999, 2000, 2002, 2003
Holman Bible Publishers

2  3  4  5  6  7  8  9  10  08  07  06  05  04

# CONTENTS

# EVIDENCE OF FAITH

## OLIVER NORTH

CAMP LANCER
HQ, 3RD BATTALION, 66TH ARMOR
4TH INFANTRY DIVISION
BAYJI, IRAQ
22 NOVEMBER 2003

When I left these soldiers nearly six months ago, they had just occupied this abandoned Iraqi Air Force Base northwest of Tikrit—Saddam Hussein's hometown. Now, because press reports have been generally full of bad news, I've returned to report for FOX News on the progress of subduing those who are opposed to freedom in Iraq.

And the evidence of great progress is here. More people in the region have electricity, clean water, and sanitation than ever before. The schools have all reopened. For the first time in history, mayors of the communities surrounding this remote U.S. Army base have all been elected. American-trained Iraqi police officers patrol streets, and neighborhoods and local Iraqis are taking responsibility for their own governance and security functions.

All of this has drawn scant attention from the U.S. media, but that's not particularly remarkable to these young troopers. One Infantry captain told me, "I'm not surprised. It's 'good news.' Most of the media just do not 'get it.'"

Unfortunately, that's not the only good news that the press doesn't "get." Many of my media colleagues seem intent on exposing some error in American strategy or tactics, confirming that troop morale is suffering or proving that our efforts to bring democracy to Iraq are fraught with failure. This focus apparently has blinded most reporters to another profoundly important aspect of the young Americans who have come to Mesopotamia to offer others the hope of freedom—their faith.

It's an interesting omission from most of the reports coming out of Operation Iraqi Freedom. None of us who were embedded for months with these remarkable young soldiers, sailors, airmen, and Marines could be unaware of it. Chaplains, chapel services, and Bible studies were—and are—much in evidence among all the units serving in this new war on terror. So, too, are the daily acts of Christian charity and compassion that are part and parcel of everyday activity for these young Americans. Yet these most fundamental and visible manifestations of Christian faith in the day-to-day lives of these warriors have largely escaped mention in the U.S. media.

That's a shame, for many of these fighters—of every rank—believe that their faithfulness to the Word of God has much to do with the success of their mission. And that mission is far more complex and difficult than many here at home perceive.

Initially, American and coalition troops had relatively simple and straightforward goals: remove Saddam Hussein from power, eliminate the threat of Iraqi weapons of mass destruction, and shut down Baghdad's support for terrorism. To achieve these ends, approximately 170,000 U.S. and British soldiers, sailors, airmen, and Marines first had to beat Saddam's 485,000-strong military. Despite gloom-and-doom prognostications from "military experts" in the U.S. media, the allied coalition accomplished all this in a lightning-swift campaign that began on 20 March and culminated with the fall of Baghdad on 10 April and the capture of Tikrit three days later.

It was an extraordinary military operation. Never before has any military force gone so far, so fast, with so few casualties—to either side—as in this campaign. No other armed forces but ours could have accomplished what these young Americans achieved. As I said on the air, reporting from Baghdad on 11 April, "Their skill and daring, discipline and endurance are without parallel in the world today." But then, having beaten the Butcher of Baghdad, the mission suddenly changed.

The warriors whose courage, stamina, and military prowess had defied the predictions found themselves in a new role: peacemakers. In many respects it's a more difficult task than simply fighting. Today our troops are charged with the responsibility of bringing democracy to a people who have known only tyranny all their lives. While rebuilding the decrepit infrastructure of an oil-rich nation, our troops must also be on guard against Baathists—remnants of Saddam's regime—who are intent on preventing real democracy from ever happening. Throughout Iraq, our soldiers have to contend with heavily armed criminals—

released from prisons by Saddam shortly before hostilities commenced in March 2003. And most dangerous of all, U.S. troops must defend against the radical Islamic Jihadists who have entered Iraq from neighboring countries intent on killing themselves in an effort to kill any "Westerner," Christian, or Jew.

Like the kamikaze pilots of World War II, the Jihadists have been taught that if they kill themselves in the act of killing an American, they will reap financial rewards for their families in this world—and spiritual rewards for themselves in the next. They are not simply *willing* to die for their cause; they *want* to die—and take as many infidels with them as possible in the process.

Western political and military leaders may say that coalition forces are not waging a religious war against Islam, but most of our troops in Iraq know that for the Jihadist suicide-bombers this is very much a religious war. The Saudi, Syrian, Egyptian, Jordanian, Somali, Sudanese, and Yemeni terrorists who blow themselves to pieces while sitting in a truck full of explosives know only hatred, how to kill others, and how to kill themselves. Their political and spiritual leaders have given them nothing to live for—only a cause that requires them to die.

Nearly all the troops with whom I have lived in Iraq understand both the military and spiritual dimension of this kind of adversary. A great number of these young Americans are believers. They know the Word of God from studying the Bible. And from biblical doctrine they know that salvation isn't a matter of how they die but how they live. For Christians, all the required dying was done on Calvary two thousand years ago.

And because they are so well grounded in their faith—

and because so many of their leaders have a personal relationship with their Lord and Savior—these young Americans have performed not only with courage but with remarkable compassion—toward one another, toward Iraqi civilians, and even toward the enemy.

Perhaps most impressive of all is the effect these young Christians are having on others whose lives they touch—overseas and here at home. Their stories are inspirational—in life and even in death.

Commander Frank Holley was the senior chaplain in the 5th Marine Regiment during Operation Iraqi Freedom. He had numerous close encounters with the kind of young Christians who so impressed me during the long fight from Kuwait to the Iraqi capital. I asked him how he dealt with the loss of so many fine young soldiers after relating to him the painful story of a Navy medical corpsman, HM3 Michael Johnson, who had been killed trying to save the life of a wounded Marine. The wounded Marine lived. The brave corpsman didn't—and his body had been brought to the helicopter on which I was flying.

Chaplain Holley replied, "Prior to leaving Kuwait, 3rd Battalion, 5th Marines' Gospel Choir, which you heard sing on Palm Sunday just outside Baghdad, provided the music for our worship services the last two Sundays before the war started. HM3 Johnson was sitting in the front row of the choir each Sunday, and on our last Sunday in Kuwait

> **"Perhaps most impressive of all is the effect these young Christians are having on others whose lives they touch—overseas and here at home. Their stories are inspirational—in life and even in death."** Oliver North

before launching the attack, he came forward for communion. My thoughts from my journal that day are as follows:

"'The last Protestant worship service on 16 March was standing room only, and as Marines and Sailors came forward for Holy Communion, I thought to myself as I administered the sacrament to each, *Lord, what will become of this man? Will I see him again if tomorrow we get the word to go? Father, may this spiritual food sustain him in the days ahead. Father, protect and watch over each of us, Your servants. Lord, I don't know what is ahead, but use me as an instrument of Your grace.'*

"It turns out that I was the last person to give him communion before his death. I distinctly remember him coming forward because that particular Sunday he needed a shave. I truly believe that the good Lord used that image of him needing a shave so I would remember him. On 30 March when I learned of his death, and that of Major Kevin Nave, the executive officer of 3/5, I traveled up to their CP to check in with the battalion CO, Sam Mundy, and see how my junior chaplain, Mark Tanis, was doing.

"I didn't know which corpsman had been killed until Chaplain Tanis told me that he was the tall African-American corpsman who sat in the front row of the choir back in Kuwait. I thought, *The guy who needed a shave.* Though we grieved his death, we were comforted by the fact that this man knew the Lord.

"But that's not all. On 17 September 2003, the Branch Medical Clinic at MCRD San Diego was named for HM2 Michael Johnson—he had been promoted to HM2 posthumously. I attended the dedication ceremony, and after it was over I was able to go up to Petty Officer Johnson's wife and parents and share some time with them. I told them with choking voice and misty eyes that I grieved when I learned of their beloved's death, that I had given him communion the last Sunday before his death, that he sang in our gospel choir, and that I hoped the assurance of his faith in Christ would bring them comfort. I also told them that their husband/son was a model of the kind of Christian courage and compassion that is so essential to our success as a nation—and that his name on the clinic would be an inspiration to others for generations to come.

"HM2 Johnson may no longer be with us in this life, but he's still being used by the Lord for a good purpose. His work isn't done. We never know how God uses us or what God has in store for us until He pronounces His work done."

Chaplain Holley's story parallels others. Lieutenant Matt Ritchie, a Marine artillery officer, was a forward observer with 2nd Tank Battalion during the attack on Baghdad. His unit was heavily engaged for days on end and sustained significant casualties. I first met him years ago at Greenbrier Christian Academy in Chesapeake, Virginia. I saw him again in the Iraqi capital and then later back in the U.S. I asked him to assess what he had been through. He replied, "I thank God for the experience. I came to know Him in a way that I never realized was possible. I now have a better understanding of what the men of the Bible went through. I always wondered about David's thoughts and emotions while he was writing about his enemies in the Psalms and about how Joshua and David felt when they lost men in battle. Being in Iraq was an experience I'll not forget. Every time I look at my pictures from over there I see the faces of those I served with—those who died and those who lived. Our national anthem has never sounded so good to me. We have been richly blessed."

These are men who have been changed by war. They see things differently than they did before they went. War, it is said, is the worst of human endeavors. It is brutal in its execution, horrific in its consequences, and searing to those it touches—be they soldier or civilian. Yet war, for all its terror and tribulation, is often a crucible in which unbreakable relationships are forged.

> **"I thank God for the experience. I came to know Him in a way that I never realized was possible. I now have a better understanding of what the men of the Bible went through. I always wondered about David's thoughts and emotions while he was writing about his enemies in the Psalms and about how Joshua and David felt when they lost men in battle. Being in Iraq was an experience I'll not forget."**
>
> **Lt. Matt Ritchie**

My father, a soldier in World War II, counted among his closest confidants and friends those with whom he served during the Battle of the Bulge. To this day, decades after we served together in the jungles of Vietnam, members of my rifle platoon and I remain devoted to one another. It has been that way for countless other soldiers, sailors, airmen, and Marines who have been thrust together in the adversity and carnage of combat. And so it is with the young Americans I have been blessed to cover in Operation Iraqi Freedom—the young Americans described in this book. They not only have a closer relationship with one another—and with this country—they also have a closer relationship with their Lord and Savior.

**"Haven't I commanded you: be strong and courageous? Do not be afraid or discouraged, for the LORD your God is with you wherever you go."** Joshua 1:9

**"** All of you—all in this generation of our military—have taken up the highest calling of history. You're defending your country and protecting the innocent from harm. And wherever you go, you carry a message of hope—a message that is ancient and ever new. In the words of the prophet Isaiah, 'To the captives, "come out,"—and to those in darkness, "be free.""**"**

**President George W. Bush**

from the deck of the USS *Abraham Lincoln* at sea off the coast of San Diego, California; May 1, 2003

The one who lives under the protection of the Most High
dwells in the shadow of the Almighty.
I will say to the LORD, "My refuge and my fortress,
my God, in whom I trust."
He Himself will deliver you from the hunter's net,
from the destructive plague.
He will cover you with His feathers;
you will take refuge under His wings.
His faithfulness will be a protective shield.
You will not fear the terror of the night,
the arrow that flies by day,
the plague that stalks in darkness,
or the pestilence that ravages at noon.
Though a thousand fall at your side
and ten thousand at your right hand,
the pestilence will not reach you.
You will only see it with your eyes
and witness the punishment of the wicked.
Because you have made the LORD—my refuge,
the Most High—your dwelling place,
no harm will come to you;
no plague will come near your tent.
For He will give His angels orders concerning you,
to protect you in all your ways.
They will support you with their hands
so that you will not strike your foot against a stone.
You will tread on the lion and the cobra;
you will trample the young lion and the serpent.
Because he is lovingly devoted to Me,
I will deliver him;
I will exalt him because he knows My name.
When he calls out to Me, I will answer him;
I will be with him in trouble.
I will rescue him and give him honor.
I will satisfy him with a long life
and show him My salvation.  **Psalm 91**

# PATRIOTISM AND FAITH

## THE *TRUMAN* AT WAR

There is a great amount of pride in serving on the USS *Harry S. Truman,* both the youngest and largest aircraft carrier in the United States fleet. But the men and women on board the *Truman* this early spring day have been at sea for almost three months without a port stop, and the repetitiveness of working twelve-hour days in narrow spaces is starting to show in the faces of the sailors.

As the ship moves somewhere through the East Mediterranean with no view of land in sight, the absence of grass, trees, and loved ones begins to unravel already thin nerves. Like the crest of a nearby wave breaking against the ship's keel, there's a restless feeling rising to the top for something—anything—to happen.

Today, the *Truman* crew will finally get their wish.

It's A-Day. Operation Iraqi Freedom has begun.

And here, like everywhere else, there's a job to do.

It's clearly a matter of defense for our families and our country.

## In the Face of War

The flight deck is normally the loudest and most active part of the ship, but it's quiet for the moment, the roar of the engines missing from the gray birds parked at the end of the ship. A backdrop of pale blue sky and one perfectly arched rainbow hangs just off the ship's bow, offering stark contrast to the unfolding drama on board as crew members walk back and forth between planes, making adjustments.

As a cool afternoon breeze slowly rolls across the deck, a group of embedded media stands in the middle of everything, taking in the sights and sounds of battle preparations.

Brown- and red-shirted sailors, responsible for the planes and the ordnance they carry, work quickly preparing the birds for their first official night of combat. The media's constant presence—a novelty and a first for a U.S. war—underscores the anticipation.

"All I know is these planes are leaving with a whole bunch of bombs and they're not coming back with them," an enthusiastic, young nineteen-year-old "brown-shirt" tells an inquiring reporter. His seasoned counterpart, an old sea dog of more than twenty years, offers a deeper perspective about the war. "It's clearly a matter of defense for our families and our country."

## Many Parts, One Mission

**"For as the body is one and has many parts, and all the parts of that body, though many, are one body—so also is Christ." 1 Cor. 12:12**

There are no unimportant jobs on board an aircraft carrier, especially during war. Everyone plays a strategic part in the success of the mission, from the airmen in various colored jerseys to the sailors below wearing different colored shirts. Each color represents a part. And each part makes all the difference.

# THE WAR
# WITHIN A WAR

Facing war, even from the decks of a ship wielding enormous firepower, always brings more to mind than the mission at hand. Thoughts of family hover close, despite the thousands of miles that separate. And for Christians and non-Christians alike, faith in God can grow or be born as mankind is reminded of his mortality and the longing for peace.

It's a longing that Commander Chaplain Doyle Dunn sees in the eyes of almost every young enlisted sailor he meets. Dunn, command chaplain for the aircraft carrier and the *Truman*'s battle group, oversees a staff of three junior chaplains and fifteen lay leaders through the ship's religious ministries department for the five thousand sailors and Marines on board.

"I see so many eighteen- and nineteen-year-old young men and women who come from broken homes and tough life experiences," Dunn reflects. "They join the military looking for a sense of purpose. This opens the door to share Jesus Christ with them. Every time I get a chance to see a sparkle of recognition in their eyes—well, that's what I live for.

## One Man's Mission

Dunn started out as an associate pastor of a sixty-member, Southern Baptist church in Harrogate, Tennessee, just down the road from his alma mater, Clearcreek Baptist College in Pineville, Kentucky. When the pastor left shortly after he arrived, Dunn was the one the church called to lead. At twenty-five, his niche seemed to be college students. Sure enough, within six months, more Clearcreek students were attending than regular church members.

"My wife and I began praying God would put me where He wanted me to be," says Dunn. "There were sixty-six churches in that county alone. I couldn't help feeling that any one of the retired pastors in the area could do what I was doing."

God soon began directing various people into the Dunns' lives who talked about the incredible ministry opportunity of a military chaplain. Dunn saw similarities in young enlisted soldiers and the college students he worked with.

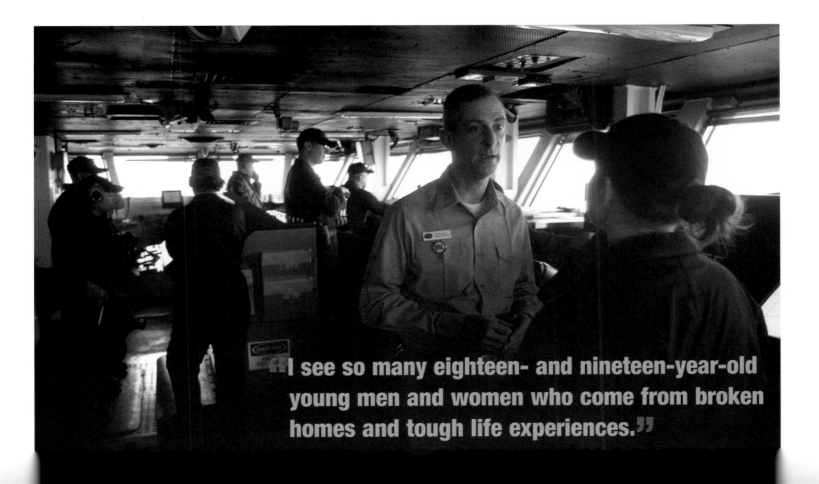

"I see so many eighteen- and nineteen-year-old young men and women who come from broken homes and tough life experiences."

"These young men and women come into the military looking for purpose in their life," says Dunn, a father of three. "This was a prime time to share with them about Jesus and the truth."

After graduating from seminary in 1987, he went straight into active duty and has served as a Navy chaplain for the last sixteen years—on both U.S. coasts, in the Gulf War, Somalia, and at the Pentagon on September 11, 2001.

This isn't the first time the chaplain has served in a war against Iraq. But it's the first time on water. During the Persian Gulf War, Dunn spent his days living and ministering to Marines deployed to Kuwait.

On the *Truman*, sailors meet for services in the chapel or in another meeting room down a corridor that takes no more than six or seven minutes to walk. Staying in touch and watching for opportunities to minister aren't hard on

board a ship. Out in the sand was a different story. Soldiers were often attached to units spread out like a mixed-up chessboard, covering miles of area. While Dunn frequently traveled to the soldiers, sometimes the troops came to him if Dunn could create a central location to meet.

One particular night, as he set up for the rare occasion of the men coming to him, Dunn felt himself growing nervous. The evening's lesson was on leadership, and he wasn't quite sure what the group's response to the visual aid would be. The Bible story for the night was about Jesus washing His disciples' feet, and Dunn wanted to make it more real for the soldiers.

Chuckling at the recollection, he remembers, "The guys had been out in the desert for weeks. No one was pulling anyone else's boots off! But the sand and wind had done a number on everyone's boots. So I was planning on picking out one of the Marines and polishing his boots for him."

Twelve Marines, mostly enlisted but a couple of officers as well, showed up for the meeting. As Dunn talked about Jesus washing the feet of His followers, he stacked cardboard MRE boxes in the middle of the circle and asked a young lance corporal—the most junior man in the group—to have a seat.

The young soldier's eyes grew wide with surprise as the chaplain slowly knelt down in front of him and began to wipe the arid desert sand and dust from one of his boots. Suddenly there was a sound behind him, and a hand touched Dunn's shoulder. It was one of the commanding officers. Taking the rag out of Dunn's hands, he tore it in half, handing back a piece to Dunn but keeping the other half for himself. Bending down, he began polishing the other boot of the lance corporal.

Whether it's new dads away from their babies, mothers missing their families, homesick eighteen-year-old sailors, or husbands with marriages crumbling back home, life goes on, even during war.

"That's really what Jesus did—He got down when He had no reason to get down," says Dunn. "The men caught the significance of that, that night."

This moment serves as a reminder of the call Dunn answered from God as a young pastor more than two decades ago. "All of these things have blended together for who I am as a chaplain," he says.

It's a calling that has led him far and wide. It's led him here to the *Truman* on this day, a scant few moments from war, aware of not only what he's about to see in the sky but discover again in the hearts of the men and women preparing to launch the attack. They need him, and he will be there.

## They need him, and he will be there.

Lieutenant Chaplain Cory Cathcart visits with a young sailor.

## A Prayer for Peace

The significance of tonight's launch is not lost on the Christians on board. They see the battle won, the regime revoked, and the Iraqi people, once oppressed under a terrible dictator, now free. Their prayers include protection for the innocent and for good to conquer evil. Most of all, they pray for peace.

And they see its potential right in front of them.

With twenty-six different faith groups living aboard the *Truman,* there is every opportunity for disagreement and strife. But Dunn says it doesn't exist.

"When I look at these groups living together in peace, it says a lot to me. It inspires me. Even if I don't agree with another's beliefs, we can still live in peace. I wish we could hold this ship up to the Arab world and say, 'Look what could be!'"

Dunn also has another wish: to hold up Jesus Christ, to declare that mankind has an even greater need than peace on earth—the peace of a heart scrubbed clean through Christ's forgiveness. The best way Dunn has learned to share this reality with others is to reflect Christ in everything he does.

"Telling people about Jesus is the number one priority," says Dunn. "But meeting their need as Jesus did is where we should start. Look how Jesus won people to Him in the Bible. He touched them where they needed to be touched."

Touching people on this ship means reaching them through their family concerns, ministering to them through their losses, helping them overcome past physical and emotional abuses by offering counseling and prayer. Whether it's new dads away from their babies, mothers missing their families, homesick eighteen-year-old sailors, or husbands with marriages crumbling back home, life goes on, even during war. There's much work for these men and women to do on ship, but there's no escaping such matters of the heart. Dunn is here to make sure these needs aren't treated lightly but rather with Christlike honesty, gentleness, and respect.

Lieutenant Chaplain Cory Cathcart, who serves under Dunn in the chaplain's corps on board the *Truman,* calls him a "pastor's pastor."

"Dunn is the real article in terms of being a servant chaplain," says Cathcart. "For a command chaplain to be involved in the lives of all the sailors is rare. Not all chaplains in his position are like that. He is truly the right man

> **"To everything there is a season, a time for every purpose under heaven. A time of war and a time of peace . . ."**
>
> **Chaplain Dunn**

for this season we're in. I really believe God ordained him to be here at this time and in the life of our ship."

The humble chaplain admits it was not his choice to come to the *Truman.* The honor of serving a ship like this is a great one, and Dunn didn't feel that he had served long enough for the position. Though he says he tried several times for an assignment elsewhere, the *Truman* is where he ended up.

"When the detailer told me this was indeed where I would be coming, I said, 'This is great,'" says Dunn. "It had absolutely nothing to do with me or my decision. I know it was God who put me here. I know it's for His purpose alone."

The spiritual role Dunn holds on ship extends beyond the enlisted sailors and officers. He also serves as an advisor on religious matters to the admiral—the first time in history for a command chaplain to perform this role.

So when the admiral announces to the ship's crew that Operation Iraqi Freedom has begun, Dunn stands right beside him, ready to offer encouragement and prayer.

Even before the initial bombs have dropped, before the first prisoners are taken, and before the first casualties of war are killed, Chaplain Dunn offers this simple prayer for all to hear on board the *Truman.*

"To everything there is a season, a time for every purpose under heaven. A time of war and a time of peace. Lord God, now we enter the season of war. For the United States and the nations that stand alongside us, this is the season to end

the dangers posed to the world by Saddam Hussein and the tyranny of his government and his military.

"Now is our season to bring liberty to the people of Iraq. To free them from oppression and to introduce to them the concept of liberty and justice for all.

"We ask, dear Lord, for a deep reservoir of strength and wisdom to carry out our mission of liberation. Help each one of us, in all our various acts, to courageously give our very best. May the actions of our forces at sea, in the air, and on land bring about a swift and undeniable victory. May the labor and sacrifice . . . in these days ahead serve to bring us through the season of war and return us safely to the season of true peace."

**"Now is our season to bring liberty to the people of Iraq. To free them from oppression and to introduce to them the concept of liberty and justice for all." Chaplain Dunn**

## Through the Night

On a ship that never slumbers, missions run continuously around the clock. The men and women aboard the *Truman* recognize the importance of what they do. It means either success or failure for the planes launching off the flight deck. Success is the only option.

"You will not fear the terror of the night, the arrow that flies by day." Psalm 91:5

## Life in a House of Steel

Twenty-four hours a day, seven days a week, these sailors work, rest, and live in a space the length of the Empire State Building on its side. Grass becomes a pleasant memory. You yearn for the day you'll feel carpet between your toes again.

# The Beginning of the End

The *Truman* now is completely dark outside except for the blinking lights twinkling from the slow-rolling planes moving into position. A full moon hovers close to the horizon, peeking out behind a cloud. With yellow reflective tape outlining their jerseys, sailors resemble glowing apparitions as they move against the pitch blackness of the flight deck. An elevator rises to the deck from somewhere below the ship, long slender missiles exposed in the crate.

Planes, with ordnance loaded, wait for the signal.

Suddenly an engine roars to life, and the wings of the first plane slowly lower into position, green lights glowing like the points of a constellation. The hand of the crew member drops, and the jet shoots off the deck, launching into the black abyss ahead.

Tonight carries the promise of "shock and awe" over Iraq. Freedom has never been closer.

# A CALLING BIGGER THAN THE NAVY

It's the first Saturday morning of the war and Keith Milo, an E4 from Bridgeport, Connecticut, and Elvin Rolon, an E3 from Orlando, Florida, nervously stand near their racks on board the *Truman*. Lieutenant Darren McFall, assistant supply officer for the aircraft carrier, is conducting an inspection of their berthing. It isn't going very well.

"The deck looks good, but there's a lot of dust up here," says McFall, taking a finger and wiping it along the top rail of a rack, revealing a large amount of black dirt.

The inspection of the "head," or rest room, doesn't go any better.

"There's a lot of lime deposit. You're going to have to come back and spend some time in here this week," the lieutenant informs the young sailors, who respond with glum faces.

On the way to the next inspection, McFall acknowledges he's pretty strict with the sailors.

"I hate being mean," he says, shaking his head. "But we hold everyone to a high standard. Living quarter conditions for enlisted are tough enough—there's not a whole lot of personal space. It's even worse if the conditions are bad. When you have good living conditions, it translates to better morale, which is good for the whole ship."

McFall is the key officer responsible for basic services on the ship, such as food and laundry. There are many areas of the ship he refers to as "his space"—ship sections that fall under his supervision. But his concern for the men extends beyond just services.

He cares about their souls too.

"The greatest thing I ever did was join the Navy," he says. He speaks passionately about the career he began almost twenty years ago. Rightly so. To McFall, it was both God and the Navy who saved his life.

## Joining Up

A baseball player in college, he'd completed almost three years of school before getting married at twenty. But things didn't go very well that first year. After opening a restaurant that quickly failed, McFall and his wife felt they were at the lowest point in their lives. That's when their church stepped in.

"I was young and full of pride; I wasn't about to let other people help me," McFall says. "So when I was out, the pastor came and paid my bills."

But the McFalls knew that help like this could only last a little while. He decided to fall back on the one thing he knew—the military. He had some experience as a reservist with the National Guard, and he saw signing up full-time as

**"I said, 'God, you must have a plan beyond my understanding.' I felt like He was saying to me, 'Just put it in My hands.'" Lt. Darren McFall**

his family's only chance for survival. Though he admits he didn't want to join the military at the time, he made a pact with God that he trusted Him to get him through.

"I said, 'God, you must have a plan beyond my understanding,'" McFall says. "I felt like He was saying to me, 'Just put it in My hands.'"

It was a decision that—looking back—the officer can see where God was leading. "I can see how I came in as a twenty-four-year-old, full of myself, and the transformation that ultimately occurred."

## Key Change

One of the biggest changes for the American-born, Mexican-raised Southern Baptist was his understanding of worship and how it would impact his calling as a Christian sailor.

Throughout his nineteen-year career in the Navy (twelve years overseas), McFall, his wife, and two sons were exposed to several small, culturally diverse churches. One Sunday during a two-year stint in the South Pacific, their family visited a small congregation while searching for a church home. Once inside, he immediately noticed a set of drums as part of the music

equipment. It was too much for McFall, who favored traditional worship styles. So the next week his family visited another church, one that offered what seemed a more suitable style for him.

"I discovered rather quickly, though, this particular church was very legalistic," McFall says. The harshness he heard in the preaching made him question his prejudices. "I believe that theology is scriptural and worship is individual. Somehow, the Lord led us back to the other church."

Still, he could barely tolerate the contemporary music and voiced his frustration and irritation more frequently at home, especially in front of his two teenage sons.

Until one Sunday.

While listening to an older gentleman in their church testify how a rather contemporary, reggae-style song from the week before spoke to his heart, "It was at that moment I said to God, 'If you can touch him, You can touch me,'" McFall recounts. From that point, his feelings changed about music styles and worship form. He dove right in, joining the choir and slowly starting his own music ministry.

## Encouraging Words

He's continuing that ministry on the decks of the *Truman.* Each week he leads a choir for the Protestant Sunday service and sees it as a tool for drawing young men and women to God.

"Every time I walk through the mess decks, I try to find a way to encourage some of these young kids," he says, frequently sitting down to eat with the enlisted nineteen- and twenty-year-olds.

"Sometimes the chaplains with their crosses on their lapels can be a little intimidating. So in my general role as an officer, it opens up opportunities for me to talk to them and invite them to the service."

McFall believes his nineteen years of Navy service is all worth it if one person comes to know Christ as a result of his witness. "The Navy isn't a life—it's a living," laughs McFall, who calls Greenbriar Baptist Church in Chesapeake Bay, Virginia, his home church. "It's part of my ministry and how God is using me. God has a plan prepared for me.

"I like to say I'm a missionary paid by the U.S. government."

*Truman* sailors do everything with excellence. Chapel services are no different. Navy men and women find time to practice, whether a skit that illustrates a sermon or music that ministers to hearts during worship.

"The Navy isn't a life—it's a living. It's part of my ministry and how God is using me. God has a plan prepared for me." Lt. Darren McFall

# FLYING ON FAITH

From the time he was only six years old, Lieutenant Johnnie "Cooter" Caldwell wanted to fly planes.

Not just any plane. This Southern Georgia boy always wanted to fly the "really fast ones."

Unlike many in life, he's achieved his childhood dream. A graduate of the Naval Academy, Caldwell is about to complete his seventh year as an aviator and his third year of flying F-18 Hornets, the nation's first strike-fighter aircraft.

It can travel up to speeds of Mach 1.8 and "pull" seven and a half times the force of gravity (7.5 "g's").

The twenty-nine-year-old pilot says there's nothing like the challenge and thrill of launching and landing on aircraft carriers.

"Every pilot out here—we've all seen *Top Gun*," he chuckles, cracking a boyish grin. His favorite type of flight is catapulting off the deck for an early morning ops mission, the sun rising just over the water's edge. "It's the biggest rush. If you weren't awake before, by the end of the stroke you are."

Caldwell deployed to the *Truman* with his squadron, the "Gunslingers" of Strike Fighter Squadron One Zero Five (VFA-105), almost four months before the war began. Although the separation from home is difficult, Caldwell believes he's where God needs him to be.

"The past month has been pretty hard as things have heated up around here," he says, referring to Operation Iraqi Freedom. "You start feeling the anxiety—not the fear—the anxiety of what you're getting ready to do. The more you let it take control, the more it overwhelms you. I pray a lot about not worrying over things."

The pilot's candor about his faith is striking, almost out of place in a job where flyboys normally talk big and walk proud, where admitting a dependence on God can be considered a weakness. But it doesn't seem to bother him, and he speaks freely—even with several of his buddies standing nearby, listening.

"I always pray whatever I do, that God would be the priority and He would be in control," he says matter-of-factly.

**"You start feeling the anxiety—not the fear—the anxiety of what you're getting ready to do. The more you let it take control, the more it overwhelms you. I pray a lot about not worrying over things.... I always pray that whatever I do, that God would be the priority and He would be in control."** Lt. Johnnie Caldwell

## Up and Down

Night missions have been Caldwell's assignment for the last seventy-two hours. He admits they bring an added stress all their own. Flying in pitch blackness and guided only by your instrument panels could raise anyone's blood pressure. But he says prayer gets him through, in multiple ways. He knows the risks he's taking for his own life each time he launches. He also realizes the gravity of what a successful mission may mean for people on the ground.

It's a reality that never travels far from his heart.

"No one should take pride in the loss of human life," Caldwell says, his tone more serious, his eyes reflecting the heavy responsibility he knows he faces with each consecutive mission. "Whatever my mission is for the day, I have to trust the leaders who've ultimately given me my mission and believe that it is in the best interest of the country. I trust God is working through our nation's leaders. I pray for the president and my other leaders quite a bit because I know their decisions directly affect me."

When his missions are complete, he finds some downtime in his stateroom. Caldwell's thoughts often turn to his wife, Tammy, his eight-year-old daughter, Hailey, and his young son, Tyler, who just had his first birthday. He gives a lot of credit to Tammy for keeping the family unit strong.

**Caldwell and his wife encourage each other not to miss a service, and he will frequently e-mail his wife about the notes he's taken from a Sunday service on board the ship or about a passage of Scripture or book he's read.**

"She pretty much lives the life of a single mom right now," Caldwell acknowledges. "When e-mail is running, we write pretty regularly. She tells me everything going on at home—like how Tyler took ten steps the other day."

## A Family of Faith

Although he asked Christ into his heart at the young age of eleven, Caldwell's priorities shifted away from church when his interest in flying hit a peak in high school. He credits his wife's influence for bringing him back into a closer walk with God.

"I went to the same church all of my life, and so when I left home for school, it was really hard to go off and find another church," he says. "But right from the first date, Tammy expected we'd go to church together. And we did."

Accountability plays a large part in the couple's relationship. They encourage each other not to miss a service, and he will frequently e-mail his wife about the notes he's taken from a Sunday service on board the ship or about a passage of Scripture or book he's read.

Their Sunday school class at London Bridge Baptist Church in Virginia Beach, Virginia, also plays a strong supporting role for Caldwell, his wife, and family by sending e-mails to him and keeping Tammy busy with fellowships and get-togethers. It feels good to know he's always on their prayer list.

He admits he thinks about death a lot more now that he's a husband and a father. But he relies on God to protect him and give him the opportunity to come back home. He's grateful for the chaplains on board who lead the services and stand by on deck when they fly out.

## Standing Tall

He is especially strengthened by the text in Ephesians 6, about putting on the whole armor of God. "It talks about your breastplate of righteousness, your shield of faith, your helmet of salvation, and the sword of the Spirit," he recalls. "It says the reason why we must take up the full armor of God is to resist the evil one, and having prepared everything, you take a stand."

His voice catches and he turns his face away. Though he's probably read this passage hundreds of times, it's obvious that saying it out loud makes a difference. A connection of what it's all about takes visible form. His suddenly moist eyes reflect the understanding of the commitment and calling he feels God has given him—however risky, however hard.

This husband of one, father of two, and defender of millions understands the feeling of patriotism and honor that comes with the commitment he has made to serve, to fight for a country that allows him the freedom to pray and worship.

He clears his throat and repeats what he just said: "It says for us to stand."

Another blink. A pause.

"I really like that."

It's hard to believe that the most junior airmen are responsible for these multimillion-dollar planes, but it's true. Plane captains, typically the youngest in the airwing, are given the enormous duty and privilege of caring for a pilot's plane. Trust plays a major factor. So does pride in their work.

Top: Plane captains Dustin Ducatte, twenty-one, from Saranac, New York (right), and Raul Duarte, twenty, from Azusa, California, pause during a flight check on Johnnie Caldwell's F-18.

Left: A plane captain is one of the last a pilot salutes before flying off the deck of the ship. It's a sign of trust and respect, one that the young airmen work very hard to deserve.

"Whatever my mission is for the day, I have to trust the leaders who've ultimately given me my mission and believe that it is in the best interest of the country. I trust that God is working through our nation's leaders. I pray for the president and my other leaders quite a bit because I know that their decisions directly affect me." Lieutenant Caldwell

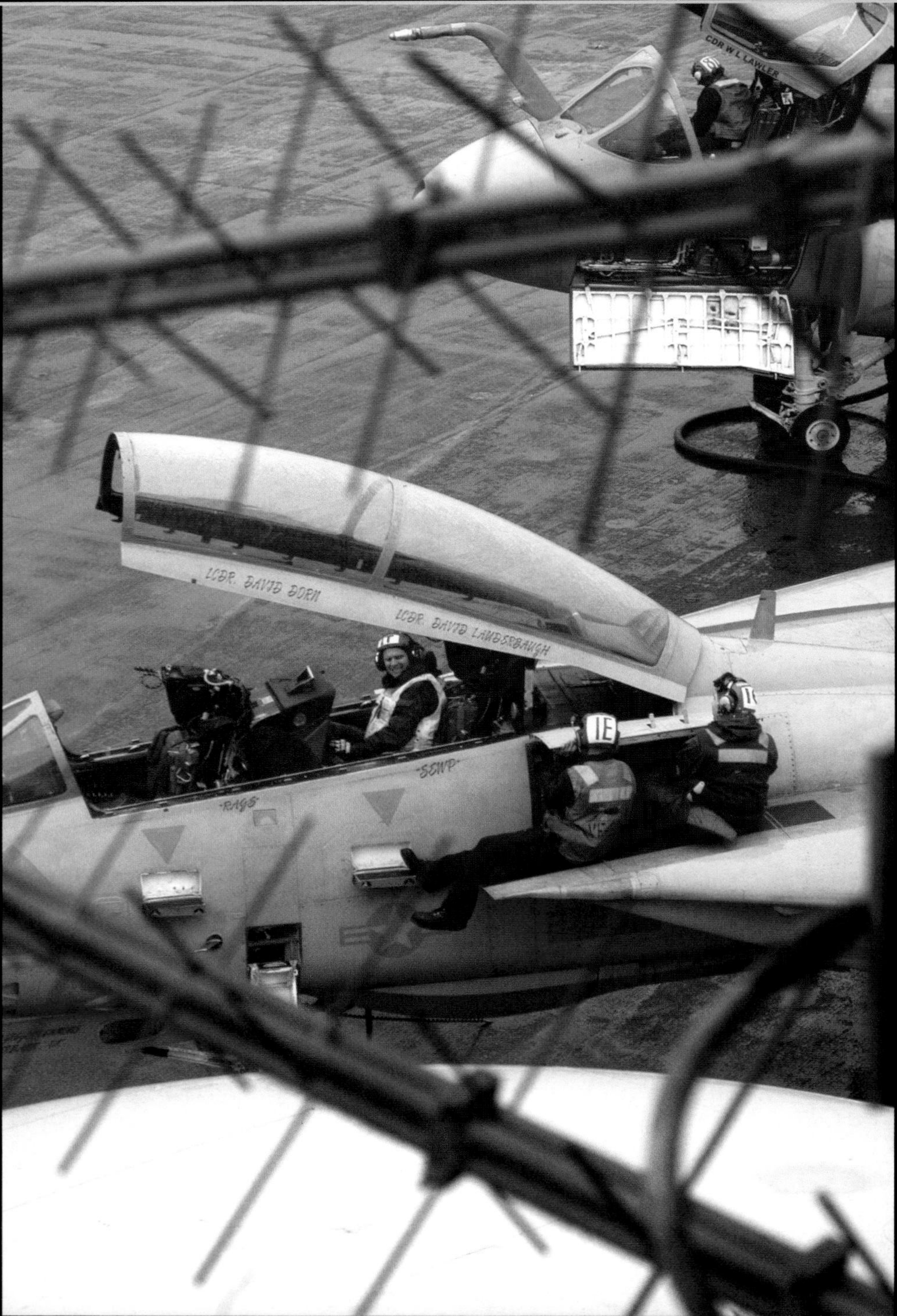
CDR W L LAWLER
LCDR. DAVID DORN
RAGS

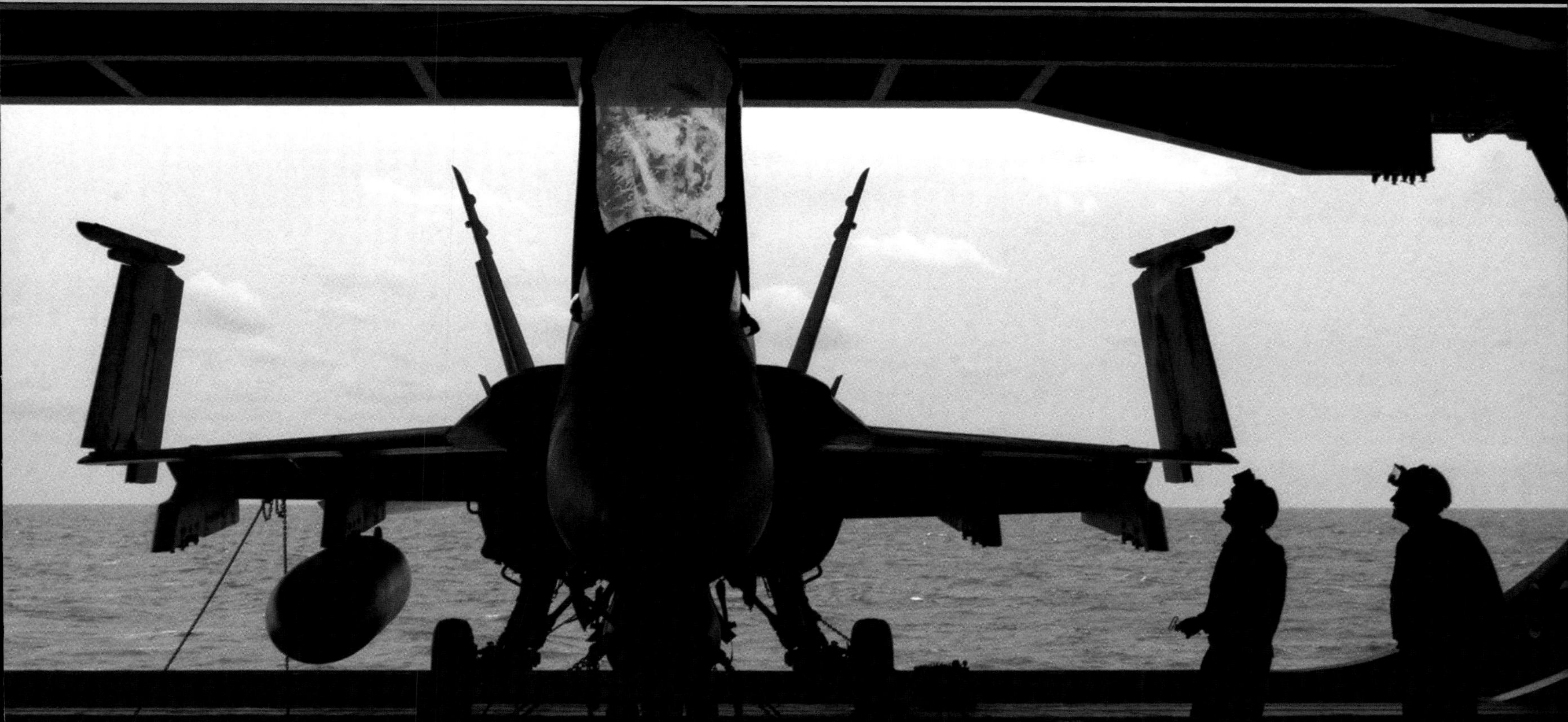

## Safe Landing

A plane comes in for a quick landing, stopping completely in under three seconds.

# MISSILE
# CRATE
# BAPTISM

Through the opening of a hangar bay door, a brilliant view of bright sunlight spills across the rolling Mediterranean waves and into the ship. It's a welcome change from high winds and heavy rains that created numerous challenges the day before.

In the middle of the hangar bay, Aviation Technician 2nd Class Sean Zahornacky, from San Jose, California, sits in a water-filled, green tub. The large container is actually a joint direct attack munitions (JDAM) crate. What once carried ordnance for destruction now serves as a vessel for an act of obedience, a symbol of a new birth and a new life.

Today the JDAM crate will serve as a baptistry—for the first-ever, full-immersion baptism on board the *Truman*.

Several excited Christians gather to watch.

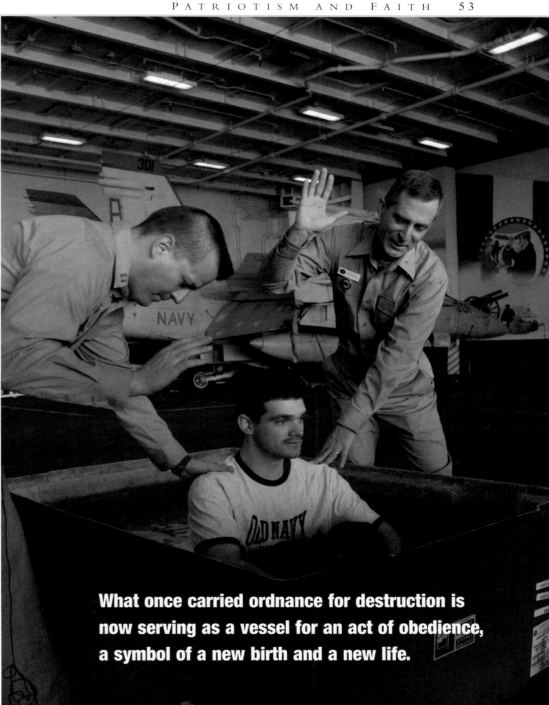

What once carried ordnance for destruction is now serving as a vessel for an act of obedience, a symbol of a new birth and a new life.

# True Conversion

Many young men and women join the Navy searching for something and ultimately find God, the chaplains say.

That's the case with Zahornacky, who has lived on the *Truman* as part of the ship's company since 1999.

He didn't have any church background growing up and admits it was very hard to come to the place of admitting he needed God. "If I don't see A and B, I don't believe C," the twenty-two-year-old says. But after many months of prayer, asking questions, and studying the Bible, he received Jesus Christ into his life.

Like many other young men, he acknowledges his girlfriend had a lot of influence. "She always went to church, but I didn't for a long time," he says. He eventually started attending with her, though reluctantly at first. "I always knew I needed a relationship with God; I just needed someone to push me."

The day he accepted Christ was one he says he'll never forget. Sitting by himself up in the fo'c'sle (the forecastle, the bow of the ship just under the flight deck), Zahornacky listened to the planes taking off overhead. Yet the pounding in his heart seemed to be decibels above what he was hearing topside. "I knew it was time to take that step of faith," he says. "It's like the 'Footprints in the Sand' poem. I could see how God was with me even through the bad times. So I just

> **"I could see how God was with me even through the bad times. So I just bowed my head and said, 'Thank You for helping me through these times. I accept You in my heart. Please help me.'"**
>
> **Sean Zahornacky**

bowed my head and said, 'Thank You for helping me through these times. I accept You in my heart. Please help me.'"

Chaplain Cory Cathcart spent a lot of time with the young sailor, sharing and making sure he understood what he was "signing up" for. The lieutenant frequently counsels young eighteen- and nineteen-year-olds experiencing their first deployment away from home—amid fifty-five hundred people on the *Truman*.

"I really believe everyone has a God-shaped vacuum inside," Cathcart said. "Many try to fill it with other things, but in the end, only God fits your heart."

Cathcart and others in the chaplain's office will be instrumental in matching Zahornacky with a couple of older mentors, encouraging him to attend church services and get involved in regular Bible studies offered throughout the week. He won't be alone.

He certainly isn't right now.

# Burial at Sea

Back on the hangar deck, Commander Chaplain Doyle Dunn lays a hand on the young man's shoulder as he explains what's about to happen. "Baptism is an event that has been celebrated for two thousand years," says Dunn. "It began in the life of Jesus, who set the example by being baptized by John the Baptist."

After a few more words and a Scripture reading by

Chaplain Cathcart, the two men prepare to lean Zahornacky back into the water.

"It is perhaps fitting that this is being done during Operation Iraqi Freedom," Dunn says. "This box is designed to bring destruction. Today, we use it to represent creation and newness of life."

The spiritual reality of this is breathtaking. Tangible.

After his baptism, the young sailor stands, wet and slightly shivering from the breeze blowing through the hangar. His fellow Christians congratulate him, and a chorus of "I Have Decided to Follow Jesus" echoes off the walls, carried out the door, into the sea air.

Perhaps the chaplain shares the feeling of everyone here: "I walk inches off the ground after something like this," Dunn says, smiling broadly. "It is such a joy to see a sailor make such a clear commitment in front of his shipmates."

Burial at sea. Life at last.

# A DIFFERENT KIND OF FIREPOWER

An aircraft carrier, wielding enormous firepower within its decks, is said to be one of the safest places in the world.

But there's another weapon wielded by Christians on board the *Truman*—the power of prayer. Intercessory prayer occurs regularly on this ship: for shipmates, for families back home, for the countries in conflict.

Lieutenant Erica Dobbs, a member of Kempsville Church of God in Virginia Beach, Virginia, is a daily part of this spiritual assault. Most noontimes, she meets with others in the chapel. Though small in numbers, their prayers are passionate. With the sounds of planes launching overhead, headed for targets unknown, these four crew members of varying rank and position pray.

They pray for the soldiers and Marines on the ground. For the POWs. For the families of those killed in action.

For the aviators and the success of their missions. For "the young children who are so confused and don't understand the meaning of war."

For everything they can think of.

## Praying without Ceasing

Dobbs is serving her twentieth year in the Navy. A wife and mother, she feels a special burden for the job she performs each day, supervising nineteen- and twenty-year-olds as they load ordnance onto the planes.

She acknowledges it's troubling.

As each missile is attached to the bottom of the great steel birds, on its way to a specific location of destruction,

"I try to lift up a prayer for those who will be in the area," she says. "I pray the innocent ones won't be harmed."

Yet she feels at peace despite the war. Growing up in Philadelphia with a mother who was a "prayer warrior," Dobbs gave her life to Christ at the age of eight. She is assured of God's protection during these days of deployment, and she sees her role in the military as a job to perform for Christ's glory.

And so the prayers of the group continue.

They voice concerns for the Iraqi people, that they may know God and His truth.

They pray for "the evil people, that they will stop killing innocent people and hurting others."

Voices are raised, seeking God's wisdom, claiming His protection and guidance for their leaders, including President Bush, the admiral, the captain.

They end their prayer, acknowledging, "It's all about Him; it's not about us."

They know that prayer is not the least thing they can do.

**"I try to lift up a prayer for those who will be in the area."** Lt. Erica Dobbs

They end their prayer,
acknowledging that
"It's all about Him;
it's not about us."

# PRAYER WALKING

They walk step by step, shoulder to shoulder, filling the width and walking the length of the flight deck as the sun rises just over the horizon of a pale blue sky. These sailors aboard the *Truman* may look like they're marching in slow motion— their heads down, their voices silent. But they're actually looking for F.O.D.—foreign object debris—material that plays havoc if sucked into a jet engine.

The FOD walk is a common drill, typically ordered by ship officers at least once if not twice a day, depending on the number of flight missions carried out. The ship chaplains can also be found participating.

But they take the walk one step further.

They walk across the 1,096 feet of flight deck, silently lifting up prayers to God for the ship's safety, for the sailors below, and for the war at large to be over—quickly, with as little loss of life as possible.

Chaplain Dunn takes the walk as often as his schedule allows. He believes the power of prayer changes the lives of the men and women aboard. He as well as other Christians and lay leaders of various Bible studies and church services have conducted the prayer walking since Dunn joined the ship as command chaplain.

"There are so many documented examples of God bringing revival to the military during war and peace times," says Dunn. "The prayer walking came as a result of discussion among the lay leaders and my staff about what it would be like if God transformed this ship.

"There's no better way to ask for that than through prayer." Through walking, living, breathing prayer.

# DOUBLE BLESSING

The birth of a child is a powerful moment to behold in a father's life . . . when you're able to behold it, that is. But military deployments often create distances too great for fathers to make it home for their child's birth. For the many new dads currently serving aboard the *Truman,* it's a moment they're missing.

Yet that didn't stop Ernest Commack from being as close as he could for the arrival of his first child.

On a ship-to-shore call to his mom's cell phone, Commack was on the line through most of his wife, Felicia's, labor back in late January 2003, two months before the United States went to war with Iraq. He reminded her about breathing tips they learned in Lamaze before he left. He told her how much he loved her. When the pain got too intense for Felicia to talk, his mom fed him updates of what was happening.

Finally, Chauncey Avidan Commack—the reason for the extra pucker in Daddy's dimple—arrived. The labor nurse held his crying newborn son near the phone for Commack to hear.

But there were no words from the big, burly sailor. He was crying too.

Commack, a thirty-eight-year-old ATP information systems technician from Birmingham, Alabama, has served with the Navy for more than eighteen years. It's obvious he doesn't take being a first-time dad for granted. He proudly subscribes to BabyCenter.com and reads everything he can about babies.

"I think it's going to be pretty weird burping him," he says, flashing a huge smile. "But I can't wait to try it."

He wields a large, white binder that hasn't left his side for the six weeks since the arrival of Chauncey (which means "church official"). It frequently comes out when he sees a friend or fellow crew member. In the binder are dozens of pictures he has printed out from his wife's e-mails. And in his heart is a whole new perspective on life—not just his son's but his own.

> **"I see life different. If I hadn't accepted Christ, I'd be so angry, especially now that I can't go home and see my little boy. But since I got saved, I've got peace."** Ernest Commack

## A Day of Miracles

Before deployment in December, Commack attended the funeral of his wife's father, killed in a tragic fire resulting from a car accident. The man never attended church. But family members soon heard of a young woman who stopped and shared Christ with him, moments before he died. A relative confirmed the account, assuring everyone Commack's father-in-law had indeed accepted Christ before he slipped away.

The idea that forgiveness could come so quickly—simply by confessing his sin—stuck with Commack. A week later, he found himself in the chaplain's office, hoping to get some questions answered.

He did.

Right then and there, the career sailor gave his life to God. "I felt like a 'bootcamp,'" says Commack, grinning. (*Bootcamp* is the term used to label brand new Navy recruits.)

He still had to tell his wife of eight years though. So he called her "the first opportunity I had, which was the following week," recalls Commack. Before he could get the words out, she stopped him from speaking and told him a couple from the church they'd been visiting—Christian Fellowship in Virginia Beach, Virginia—had shared Christ with her as well. She, too, had become a Christian.

A couple of questions later, Commack put the pieces together. "Honey, you're not going to believe this," he remembers saying.

He and his wife were saved on the very same day.

## Thinking of Home

Since becoming a Christian, Commack regularly attends the ship's weekly gospel church service, along with a five-man Bible study.

"It's 360 degrees," he says. "I see life different. If I hadn't accepted Christ, I'd be so angry, especially now that I can't go home and see my little boy. But since I got saved, I've got peace."

The new dad is due for shore leave in only a few short weeks and plans to retire in two years. He's looking forward to the time he can spend with his new son and his thirteen-year-old stepson. He plans on teaching his boys about respect and responsibility, making sure they learn that working hard and helping people is more valuable than money. The Southern-born sailor also plans on passing down a few of his favorite, old-fashioned, Alabama values to his children—huntin' and fishin'.

It's a chance he has only one explanation for. "I give God all the credit for everything," he says. "He blessed me with a family and now a son."

## Change of Pace

Sailors take sanctuary in the ship's library, which also serves as a place to unwind from the hectic hours.
Most will be back on duty before the movie they're watching ends.

# MOMS AT SEA

It's hard to be away from your children. Whether you're a father or a mother, when your country calls for your service, you know you're missing something back home. A first loose tooth. A scraped knee you aren't there to kiss. Maybe even a first step.

Business trips are one thing. But six-month deployments are quite different.

## Missing the Action

As the war with Iraq enters its second full week, moms on board the *Truman* remain committed to the job at hand while missing their kids at the same time.

Disbursing officer Chief Nancy McNeil from Chesapeake, Virginia, spends a lot of time showing friends the latest pictures of her two small sons, seven and three. With almost twenty years in the Navy, the petite brunette admits it's hard to be away from them, but she feels blessed to be where she is.

"The people who founded our country were God-loving," says McNeil, who attends Fairview Baptist Church in Chesapeake. "I count it a real privilege for me to follow in their footsteps."

This is the longest amount of time (three months) that she's ever been away from her boys and her husband, who is also active Navy, stationed on shore. Before this deployment, she, too, was stationed on shore for six years.

"I miss my family terribly," admits McNeil, "but I have the neatest job in the Navy. As a chief I get to help train and

mold the junior officers here on board who will eventually be admirals. It's a lot like holding your baby for the first time. It's a great feeling, but what a sense of responsibility."

Lieutenant Commander Brenda Malone is the PAO (Public Affairs Officer) on board the *Truman*. This is her first deployment since joining the Navy more than eleven years ago. Though she agrees it's very hard being away from her three-year-old daughter and one-year-old son, she jumped at the two-year opportunity.

"I negotiated for two years to come to this ship," says Malone, pointing out the strong reputation that the *Truman* holds within the Naval Fleet. "I really wanted to be a part of it."

She and her husband, Anthony, are members of First Baptist Church in Norfolk, Virginia, where he works as an insurance agent.

"I know it's more traditional for moms to be at home, but my husband has taken the responsibility right now, and

he's absolutely wonderful with our kids," says Malone. "We're both professionals, and we knew we were going to have to work together."

Malone sees this time away as important not only for her but for her family's future as well. It's hard to miss the milestones of her young children—walking, talking, all the firsts, and the lasting memories. But she calls home as often as she can for updates. The workers in the day-care center where her children attend e-mail her regularly with photos and progress reports.

She also relies on a whole network of other moms on board ship to help when she's missing her kids. "We talk about how smart they are and how fast they're growing up," she says, chuckling at the bragging sessions she and her friends share as moms. "We're all going through the same struggles. It's great to have that support."

Her scheduled tour of duty isn't up until July 2004. That's a lot of time away from her home, her husband, her family. Dedication alone keeps her going.

"I want my daughter to see that if she puts her mind to it, she can do anything and succeed," said Malone. "That's how I feel about where I am right now. I'm at peace."

**"I want my daughter to see that if she puts her mind to it, she can do anything and succeed. That's how I feel about where I am right now. I'm at peace."**

**Lt. Cdr. Brenda Malone**

**Disbursing officer Chief Nancy McNeil shows a fellow coworker pictures of her husband and children she's just received from home.**

## Women at Work
Whether a ship's nurse or a navigator for fighter planes, women offer an important contribution to today's military.

# FRIENDS IN WAR

God answers prayers in the most unlikely places. For Sam Horne, it was in the jet engine shop of the *Truman.*

Horne, a young jet engine mechanic and AD aviation machinist from Williamson, South Carolina, signed up for the Navy when he was only eighteen. He had run with the wrong crowd and was out of options for his future. Longing for a sense of purpose, he decided he'd try to find it in the military.

He found more than just a career.

"After my first deployment, I wanted to find a church to go to, and since we'd been sent back to the shipyards for some downtime, I thought this would be a good time to do that," says Horne, now twenty-two.

Despite the challenge of being sent away for various training periods, Horne found a church home at Virginia Beach Freewill Baptist Church and recommitted his life to God.

"I found out what I was really longing for—a true, committed relationship with God," the young sailor says with a smile on his face.

His life didn't get any easier though. Loneliness quickly set in when he decided he shouldn't go out drinking with other sailors on base. He prayed God would send him a best friend, someone who'd understand, someone who could encourage him in his Christian walk.

That's when Horne met Chris Huggins, a guy from Bangs, Texas, who likewise worked in the jet engine shop. Discovering they were the same age and members of the same church, the two hit it off from the start, even helping as volunteer youth leaders in their congregation. Now deployed a world away from Virginia Beach Freewill, they're still keeping up with youth members through e-mail messages. Names and prayer requests from the kids are listed on a sheet of paper, taped up on one of the cabinet doors in the shop.

Yes, prayers are still being asked and answered . . . in the most unlikely places.

> **"You know the saying, 'Sleep with dogs and wake up with fleas'? If you can stay with the Vine and He stays with you, you can bear fruit. But sometimes the Vine can seem pretty far away."** Sam Horne

## Good Connections

Horne is persistent in his studies of God's Word while on board the *Truman*. He's taken the Religion 201 class offered through the chaplain's department, and he's a big fan of Focus on the Family videos and books by Max Lucado.

There are still struggles to overcome though.

"Every day you have to wake up, and sometimes you don't feel good," the young man admits. "I'm always battling in my mind to try and make sure I treat people with love and kindness.

"You know the phrase 'Sleep with dogs and wake up with fleas'?" he asks. "If you can stay with the Vine and He stays with you, you can bear fruit. But sometimes the Vine can seem pretty far away."

Horne and Huggins rely on their church's support as one way to make the time pass. Church members send cards, CDs of the pastor's sermons, and care packages that include Bible studies and whatever else the young Christians want. They also get e-mails from the associate pastor, though as of late e-mail for the ship's sailors has not been nearly as accessible. Necessary war restrictions.

But they know their church is there. Praying. Just as they are.

Sam Horne, left, and Chris Huggins monitor an engine test.

"We prayed the other night [before the first planes with loaded missiles took off] for our enemies," says Horne. "They need to see what we see. I need to see what they see. All I can do is pray. I'm not here to kill anybody—just to defend good from evil.

## Always on Call

"I think what I'm doing here is making a difference and fulfilling God's will," says Horne, displaying a wisdom that seems beyond his years. "Saddam Hussein shows a lot of hatred. The Iraqi people need to see a different part—the New Testament if you will."

They're making sure the people on board their ship are seeing it too. At lunch, Huggins ran across someone struggling to cope. What Huggins didn't realize was his fellow sailor was truly contemplating suicide, as close as five minutes away from walking off the deck of the ship, hoping to die.

Huggins shared with the sailor what the Bible said. "I told him you have a choice right now of who you will serve," says Huggins. "He chose to step up, just started bawling right there on the mess deck and gave his life to God."

If it hadn't been for Huggins sharing the love of God with him (the man later told the chaplain, with Huggins in the room), it would have been too late.

"I definitely know we're here for a reason," says Huggins, getting back to work on one of the jet engines in the shop. "I've seen it firsthand."

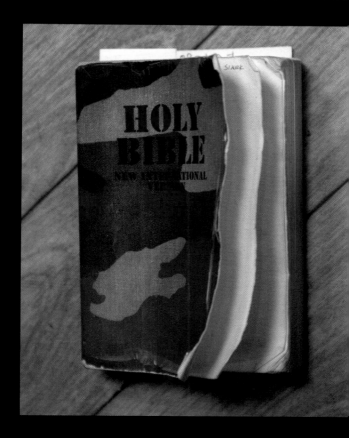

**"I told him that you have a choice right now of who you will serve. He chose to step up, just started bawling right there on the mess deck and gave his life to God."** Chris Huggins

## Bible Study

Finding time to study the Bible isn't hard to do on board a floating vessel. For many, it's a welcome distraction and opportunity to grow in faith. Whether Sunday school just like back home (left) or Bible study groups (right), sailors discover they can experience God anywhere—even in the middle of the East Med.

**"** For where two or three are gathered together in My name, I am there among them. **"** Matthew 18:20

Wade Melton (left), a member of St. Nicholas Greek Orthodox in Virginia, Fransisco Jusino (center) of Detroit, Michigan, and Mark Stark, a member of Providence Road Church of Christ in Texas talk about a Bible study they recently went through, which Stark led. Shortly before the study began, Jusino gave his life to Christ while on the *Truman*.

# SUNDAY

A deployed sailor's life leaves a lot to be desired.

The five thousand sailors and Marines on board the *Truman* don't have a lot of downtime. The young enlisted men and women typically work seven days a week, twelve hours a day at their various responsibilities and tasks. For officers it can be eighteen hours a day, overseeing and managing the enlisted. Many look forward to Sunday services led by ship chaplains and the fresh encouragement that gets them through another long, intense week.

Like this week—the second week of the Iraqi War.

Five services are offered throughout the day on any given Sunday. A Protestant liturgical service, a contemporary Protestant worship service, a gospel service, and two Catholic masses are available for sailors of all denominations and faiths. Many take advantage of the opportunity to worship.

# A Message to the Troops

More than twenty-five men and women sit in the small chapel within the decks of the *Truman,* participating in the Protestant liturgical service given by airwing Chaplain Alan Wilmot. They recite the Lord's Prayer, the Apostles' Creed, and sing the Doxology.

For general observers, this might seem like a typical Sunday service. But look closer and you'll notice several green jumpsuits with wings and the word *Gunslingers* on the uniforms. These are some of the Navy's finest—airwing pilots—men and women who flew the first air strikes into western Iraq in just the past forty-eight hours. They come for energy, for comfort, for encouragement. Many come just to pray.

Even the brave know they need it. They know they need God.

"Is our attack of Iraq a righteous one?" Chaplain Wilmot asks those in attendance. "It's all about the motivation."

Motive can be the difference between completing a mission in terms of hate or in terms of defense, he says. Doing something—anything—in hate or anger, even bombing a tyrant's regime, isn't the right reason.

Quoting Ephesians 4:26 and James 1:19–20, Wilmot encourages the group not to let anger get out of control. Anger usually is negative and counterproductive, he says, but if focused on evil and the defense of others, anger can be healthy, positive.

"Saddam Hussein is a nasty individual, but is it OK to hate him?" Wilmot asks, his listeners' faces solid, serious, silent. "We need to hate what Hussein does and how he treats his people but not him. Hate poisons us. The hate will only destroy you."

He uses the comparative example of someone who kills another person on purpose and a police officer who kills as a result of defending another life. "It's the moral difference," explains Wilmot. "I thank God that someone's willing to protect our families while we're deployed.

"It's what we're doing here for all American families."

**Motive can be the difference between completing a mission in terms of hate or in terms of defense. Doing something— anything—in hate or anger, even bombing a tyrant's regime, isn't the right reason.**

## Second Service

The contemporary Protestant service, offered at 1000 (ten-hundred), is in full swing in the fo'c'sle. More than 120 people are gathered on this particular morning, singing joyfully and enthusiastically with the praise team led by a ship supply officer.

Many raise their hands and close their eyes, as the catapults above launch another group of planes for short mission training flights. The sudden engine roars and bone-crunching thuds offer a not-so-subtle reminder that Sundays, unfortunately, aren't days of rest for everyone.

Chaplain Commander Doyle Dunn gives the week's sermon. He talks about Peter stepping out of the boat to be with Jesus.

"We've all felt fear, and we give it lots of different titles: apprehension, anxiety. There's a lot of fear out there. Having courage doesn't mean you've conquered every fear, but holding on to fear keeps us frozen in place. It keeps us from doing basic things to survive."

Courage means taking fear and pushing ahead in spite of it, Dunn explains. "Courage is a discipline—a mental muscle that cuts a path through fear."

These are messages that mean something, messages that are sure to be challenged by the rigors of the days ahead.

Cherished by those who have the courage to live them.

Many raise their hands and close their eyes, even as the catapults above launch another group of planes for short mission training flights.

## Defending the Perimeter, Protecting the Core

From the *Truman,* hundreds of miles away, to the center of Baghdad, God is visible in the hearts and lives of many in this war for freedom and democracy.

## Arriving at BIAP
**Baghdad International Airport**

Most troops entering and leaving Baghdad come through BIAP, a dusty, grimy landscape filled with sounds of jet engines and the smells of motor oil and exhaust fumes. Whether coming or going, the initial quick pace is overtaken by hours of standing by and waiting. For rides. For supplies. For home.

# THE MINISTRY OF PRESENCE

## A CHAPLAIN'S ROLE

They are soldiers, just like the men and women they serve. In fact, they've maneuvered in and around the American battlefield since the days of the Revolutionary War. But their mission has always been against a different kind of enemy. They don't carry weapons of steel and fire. They are armed instead with prayers for the wounded, counseling for the weary, and encouragement for the worried—duties that are often the difference between a soldier giving up or continuing the fight.

They are military chaplains. And many times their job is just to be there.

It's so important, they even have a name for it: "the ministry of presence."

# BEING THERE

War isn't easy to talk about. "It's almost a sacred thing in some respects," Chaplain Doug Carver says, sitting in his office, one of many rooms in what used to be Saddam's governmental palace in Baghdad. He speaks softly, reflectively, but his voice still carries, bouncing off the marble walls.

He thinks of his World War II veteran father who was uncomfortable talking about his own military memories. "There are things you see in war, things you experience, that you almost don't want to talk about except with those who have been through it as well."

Chaplain Carver knows. He has been through it. With them.

## Life in the Desert

Serving off and on in the Army since 1973, this is Carver's second war, his first to deploy. During Desert Storm, his theater of operations was far from the front, assisting families on base in Manheim, Germany. This time, he's the highest-ranking chaplain in Iraq, positioned at the heart of the battlefield and responsible (at the height of the war) for 350 chaplains and the same number of assistants.

Think of Chaplain Carver as being the senior pastor of a mammoth-sized church, except America has never seen a church like this: composed of both Christians and non-Christians, its worshipers dressed on Sunday in their desert fatigues, spread en masse across a parched and grimy desert landscape. The Sunday before the war began was standing room only inside the enormous service tent, with dozens of others straining to listen outside.

He reflects on those first days of the war, still fresh in his mind. When the first missile attack began, Carver scrambled like everyone else to pull on his chemical protection suit, gas mask, gloves, and boots. As he half-walked, half-ran to the bunker, he remembered something his wife said to him months before, after he'd complained about the bulkiness of the suit and the almost claustrophobic feeling he had during training.

"My wife said, 'I'm going to pray that when you put that stuff on, God sings to you. Just imagine you're in God's garden and He is walking with you.'"

So as he sat elbow to elbow with other soldiers in a packed bunker, laboring to catch his breath, listening for incoming rounds, the words of the old hymn drifted through his mind—*"And He walks with me, and He talks with me, and He tells me I am His own."*

"At that point there was a peace that came over me that has really stayed with me the whole time," says Carver. "I haven't been in harm's way like a lot of the young troops out there, but when you're dealing with an asymmetrical

> **"There are things you see in war, things you experience, that you almost don't want to talk about except with those who have been through it as well."**
>
> **Chaplain Doug Carver**

**"When you're dealing with an assymetrical battlefield, there is no place where you're really safe. Anything is a target."**

**Lieutenant Carver**

battlefield, there is no place where you're really safe. Anything is a target."

Carver remembers the day his convoy prepared to make the two-day, six-hundred-mile trip from Kuwait to Baghdad in the early part of April. Another chaplain brought out bookmarks printed with Psalm 91 and passed them out to the troops. This biblical prayer of protection against "the terror of the night" and "the arrow that flies by day" has long guided soldiers down the treacherous road of the unknown, much like the dusty, bleak desert highway their Humvees were about to travel.

Many miles and hours later, as their convoy moved closer to the Iraqi border, Carver noticed he was no longer seeing any civilian vehicles. He said a prayer for the troops at the last checkpoint before entering the country, before crossing into the theater, past buildings that were empty, strangely vacant. Signs along the roadside read "Entering Iraq—No Photos." This was it. This was real.

Knowing this feeling firsthand is part of what it means to be there.

## All You've Got

Experience something often enough and even the shocking becomes strangely familiar. Yet no one ever gets totally accustomed to the faces of war.

Shortly after arriving in Baghdad, Carver lived in one of the terminals at Baghdad International Airport (BIAP). The city had been taken, but there were still frequent attacks and mortar rounds—like the ordinary blast Carver heard one particular morning, the explosion not even causing him to look up from his coffee or break off the conversation he was having. Then suddenly, a real interruption—instructions to put on their flak vests and Kevlar helmets. They had "incoming."

Then, less than a minute, another request: "Chaplain, we need you."

Carver followed the soldier summoning him outside. He saw the Bradley vehicle first. The Bradley's gun had misfired, and the two soldiers standing in front of it now lay on the ground. One soldier was dead. Only a pool of blood remained as his limp body was carried away. The other soldier looked fine. Until they rolled him over. He was missing his face.

"I just remember walking with him to the aid station and watching these courageous medics frantically trying to save his life," says Carver. "Baghdad had fallen, and it just seemed like such an untimely death for a kid I'd just greeted and shaken his hand. Here, thirty minutes later, he's dead.

"That was—that was tough, seeing that."

While situations such as these have been hard to take, Carver, a Southern Baptist from the hills of North Georgia, says his faith has grown through this kind of testing.

"There's an old saying: 'You never know Jesus is all you need until He's all you've got,'" he says.

"I've learned that's true. I don't have my wife here, my children, my personal things," he says. "It's just been an army cot in a corner. It's very hard finding that quiet place. There are so many people . . . so many needs."

Yet he finds comfort in the fact that soldiers are meeting Christ. Carver has preached every Sunday since the deployment began. His sermons are "meatier," he says, inspired only by

It's very hard finding that quiet place. There are so many people . . . so many needs."

Lieutenant Carver

the Lord, by the gravity of his experiences, and by the biblically rich environment he's found himself in.

"We're living in the land where most of the prophets walked, wrote their books, and prayed," Carver says. "Ezekiel is buried here, an hour away. Daniel was confined here and helped run this country. He wrote his book here.

"Nahum, Haggai, and Isaiah walked this land. Jonah was up north in Nineveh, near the Mosul area. In Genesis 4 it says Adam's grandson began to call on the name of the Lord, here in this land."

Like other chaplains, Carver is excited about the spiritual growth he sees in the soldiers around him—men and women who are reading their Bibles in their spare time and holding Bible studies.

"This isn't some foxhole faith," Carver says. "People are growing. They get it."

That's because Jesus *is* all they've got.

## Serving God in Baghdad

Sara Brinkley, twenty, wanted to serve God. She thought she'd go to Bible school and become a pastor. Instead, she joined the Army.

A member of River of Life Open Bible Church in Spokane, Washington, the E2 serves as a cook in her unit, which is stationed at Baghdad International Airport, part of the 1st Armored Division.

"I see everyone twice a day because of my job, and I just know my presence here helps make an impact," says Brinkley, who says her ministry is encouraging other soldiers.

She admits she didn't always see it that way. When she first arrived in Baghdad, she begged her chaplain to let her help at the nearby orphanage.

"I told him I wanted to make a difference, and he said I was already doing that right where I was," she remembers.

"It's not about the big things—it's the small things that count. I can tell someone, Yeah, it's hard out here, but there's Someone who loves you."

# SOMEONE TO WATCH OVER ME

Meeting Chaplain (Major) Kevin Wilkinson is like meeting a friend you didn't know you had. Kind eyes and a broad smile are part of the uniform for this former Tennessee pastor. His quick, witty words are endearing. You might even swear he could be a politician. He almost was. He thought once or twice about making a run for a Metro Council seat back in Nashville.

But that was before his country called for him.

## A Long Road to Baghdad

Wilkinson is a chaplain serving with the 168th MP (Military Police) Battalion out of Lebanon, Tennessee. He's a reservist with the Army National Guard, one of many reserve chaplains stationed in Iraq. It is perhaps his unique background that gives his ministry such a special flavor.

There isn't a lot this chaplain hasn't done. He pastored a small Presbyterian church in northern Tennessee for twelve years. For ten of those years, he simultaneously served as pastor to a small independent church in the same area. In the 1980s he worked as a marketing rep with IBM, and toward the end of that decade, he owned his own computer company.

But he left the business world with the idea of going into military ministry, heavily influenced by a father who was career Navy and a business partner who was an admiral in the Navy Reserves. After selling his share of the company to his partner, Wilkinson attempted to get into the Navy as an active duty officer, but because of his age (thirty-eight) he was denied.

So he joined the Reserves—and has lived it to the fullest for almost thirteen years.

It wasn't without a little fear and anxiety that he made the journey to Baghdad in the middle of May. Though his unit missed the initial combat phase of the war, Wilkinson says his fear of the unknown was the one thing he dealt with more than anything else. Now that several months have passed, much of the unknown has become commonplace. "I know just what to be afraid of—and there's plenty of it!" he says, half chuckling, half serious.

He's made a cozy little residence here in the sand and coffee-colored gravel of the forward operations base (FOB) that borders the southern perimeter of Baghdad. Only one large vertical board divides the two compartments of his tent—one side his living quarters; the other, his chapel.

From his living area—bedroom, kitchen, and living room all neatly rolled into one—he can glance through the makeshift doorway that leads into the chapel, lined with four rows of chairs and a podium in the corner. He built most of it himself, including the wooden slatted walkway leading to his "front door," a tent flap. Yet it feels strangely like a home, and Wilkinson looks at home in it. His sanctuary also has become a home for many a young man's broken heart, a father's worried tone, or a soldier's pain over losing his buddy.

Death, of course, is the hardest part of the job. While it's something Wilkinson never gets used to, it is something he's very familiar with. Years ago as a seminary student, he worked at a funeral home to make extra money. By his own

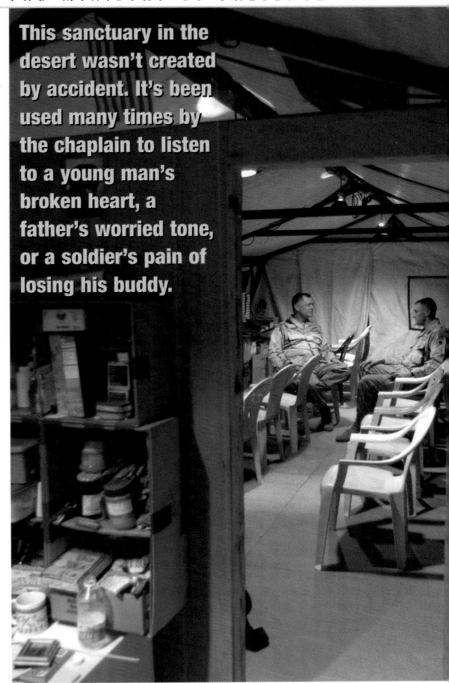

This sanctuary in the desert wasn't created by accident. It's been used many times by the chaplain to listen to a young man's broken heart, a father's worried tone, or a soldier's pain of losing his buddy.

count, he's helped more than two thousand families through the loss of a loved one. He's seen human remains in every distorted form imaginable. And though it never gets any easier to lose a soldier—especially one of his MPs—he knows the importance of being a "presence," a comfort to those impacted by the crisis of war and the death of a friend.

Like the other chaplains, "being there" is a major part of his ministry.

## God Watches the F.O.B.

He was "there" the first day of Ramadan, when a truck loaded with explosives drove up the steps of an Iraqi police station and detonated. The force of the blast destroyed forty cars parked on the street in front of the building and blew every door off its hinges inside.

"When people experience devastation of that magnitude, it has a peculiar effect," Wilkinson explains. After identifying the body of a young MP killed on the scene, he spent the rest of that day making eye contact with the soldiers he served, asking them how they were doing, ensuring they were OK.

One of the soldiers he saw was the best friend of the man he'd just identified in the morgue. "Inconsolable," he remembers, watching as other soldiers from their unit surrounded the distraught MP, hugging him, sharing his tears and his pain.

Although such scenes are difficult to go through, and the loss of a life is a hard thing to accept, Wilkinson says he's never once questioned his faith in the thirty-two years he's been a Christian.

Yet there was a day recently when he at least questioned what God was up to.

"I said, 'Lord, I've lifted up my eyes, and this isn't a field white to harvest,'" paraphrasing from Jesus' statement to His disciples in John 4:35. All Wilkinson could see in his military mission field was "a patch"—and one that was "overgrown" at that!

But he felt God rebuke him in his discouragement, reminding him to look back, to measure His faithfulness. *What about the low number of casualties?* God seemed to be asking. *What about the successes his unit experienced?*

As if to make His case more plain, a knock soon came to Wilkinson's door. It was ten o'clock at night. A young soldier, just standing there.

"Sir," he said. "I want to be saved. Can you do that for me?"

"I looked at him and said, 'Well, no son, I can't do that for you. But you've definitely come to the right place,'" the chaplain recalls, his face beaming with the memory of the young man who accepted Christ that night in his tent. He later baptized him in an improvised baptismal, with forty fellow Christians looking on to celebrate.

"I have seen the hand of God. Before, I just wasn't looking properly," Wilkinson says. "It is a field white to harvest."

It's also a field under God's constant protection.

He quotes close-to-perfect a portion of Psalm 127: "Unless the Lord builds a house, its builders labor over it in vain; unless the Lord watches over a city, the watchman stays alert in vain. Certainly He gives sleep to the one He loves."

Then—to illustrate—he pulls out a white container from a corner of his tiny room. Opening it, he reveals several remnants of a fragmented mortar shell.

"This is from the first mortar attack we experienced," he says, smiling as he holds the shell in his hand. "There were six rounds altogether, but only two reached our camp. One fell in the mud, and this one struck just seventy-five feet from the building and disintegrated instead of detonating.

"Just a few feet off and it would have punched a hole in the ceiling of a company's tent," while they were sleeping.

As he gently places the mortar pieces back into their container, he smiles brightly, almost a twinkle in his eye. "So unless God watches the FOB, these guys stay awake at night.

"But our God is an awesome God, and He is watching over us."

While destruction from the war is still evident, it's also clear the precision of the weapons used. Thanks to sophisticated technology, collateral damage remained minimal. These windows are directly above and below each other. One was hit—the other remained intact.

**"Unless the LORD builds a house, its builders labor over it in vain;**
**unless the LORD watches over a city, the watchman stays alert in vain."** Psalm 127:1

# WORTH IT

Chaplain (Major) Dan Wackerhagen believes he has the best job in the world. As an Airborne chaplain in the Army, he says he "gets to jump out of planes, tell people about Jesus—and they pay me for it!"

Like many, he was a soldier himself before he surrendered to ministry—by his own admission a "tactically, technically proficient infantry soldier." But this Southern Baptist-endorsed chaplain also admits to living a "wild, immoral life" in his early years as an enlisted man.

That's why he knows firsthand the value of a chaplain to a soldier. It was a chaplain who led him to Christ, a decision that completely changed his life.

For the better.

## "I Believe in What We're Doing"

Several years after his conversion, after going through college and receiving an officer's commission through ROTC, Wackerhagen felt called to the preaching ministry.

"While I was in seminary, the Lord laid it on my heart that He could use me to minister to soldiers," he says. "It made sense—sort of took me full circle from where I started"—back to the day when he gave his life to Christ in the office of a chaplain.

Sixteen years later, the chaplain finds himself in the most important moment of his ministry. He serves as commanding chaplain for the tens of thousands of men and women stationed at BIAP, overseeing thirty-five chaplains and sixty various services on base. It's a challenging task, but one he is committed to seeing through.

"My faith is continually made stronger by the soldiers here," says Wackerhagen, sitting in a small, brand-new white chapel after a service. "I'm inspired daily by the spirit they have and their willingness to make sacrifices. I believe in what we're doing to stop terrorism. Any doubt in my mind was erased the first few weeks we were here."

Not that he hasn't had good reason to doubt. After a Chinook helicopter went down—one of the worst accidents involving U.S. soldiers in the early going of the war—Wackerhagen himself was part of the team responsible for seeing the dead soldiers out of the country.

It's one of the toughest memories he has.

This is a man who has jumped out of C-130s more than a hundred times. He's used to seeing young, excited paratroopers on board, itching to go.

But as he watched eighteen black body bags lie in state, all he could do was utter a somber prayer for the families waiting back home.

"There's a lot of people hurting here," he admits. "A lot of people think the longer you serve in the Army, the easier it must get. I think it actually gets tougher."

He knows Operation Iraqi Freedom comes at a huge price—to these men, to these families, to himself as well. He missed his daughter's high school graduation and the start of her freshman year in college. His older son will graduate from college soon with an officer's commission—without Dad there to celebrate. The son he has seen recently—his younger boy, a National Guard reservist who received activation orders the same time his father did—is serving in Fallujah, considered a hot spot for violence by Iraqi insurgents.

Even with all this—the up-close pain of death, the homesickness for family, the added stress of having a son serving in the war—Wackerhagen believes in what he and the thousands of other soldiers are here for.

"What's going on in Baghdad can happen anywhere," he says. "We're at a focal point for global terrorism. This is worth it. It's worth it for me, for my son who's serving his country."

Freedom costs. For some, more than others. And chaplains like Dan Wackerhagen are paying the price with pride, praying "every day that God gives us the victory."

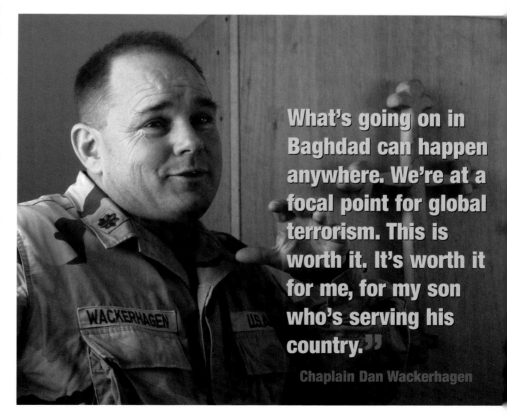

What's going on in Baghdad can happen anywhere. We're at a focal point for global terrorism. This is worth it. It's worth it for me, for my son who's serving his country."

Chaplain Dan Wackerhagen

# SEND ME

## ON THE ROAD WITH THE FALCON BRIGADE

"**I** heard the voice of the Lord saying: Who should I send? Who will go for Us? I said: Here I am. Send me." *Isaiah 6:8*

Here I am. Send me.

Rarely do five little words carry so much force and weight. Put together, these five words—all single syllables, just thirteen letters—form one of life's ultimate statements of commitment, honor, sacrifice, and selflessness. These are words that are hard to mean, hard to misunderstand. To speak these words is to know you're committing to something bigger than yourself.

Yet this centuries-old pledge is a testimony to everything the men of the 325th Airborne Infantry Regiment Falcon Brigade stand for—so central to their mission that they've posted this verse from Isaiah 6 on the home page of their Web site. It's a cyber reminder of what their job means both to themselves and the country they serve.

The 3rd Battalion is one of three in the Falcon Brigade, paratroopers who are part of the 2nd Brigade Combat Team of the 82nd Airborne Division housed out of Fort Bragg in Fayetteville, North Carolina. They're continuing the brave legacy of a long line of heroes who, since 1917, have worn the 82nd's famous "AA" (All-Americans) shoulder patch. Now stationed in Baghdad, this battalion is attached to the 1st Armored Division and is one of the first units to complete a one-year tour in Iraq.

It's been a long year.

"**We could tell a difference when the people back home were praying for us and when they weren't. It was night and day.**"

Major Jim Murphy

# MAKING A DIFFERENCE

Ten years ago, just three days away from combat in the Gulf War, Jim Murphy's mind was on his duty, his training . . . and the unsettling assurance that if he died he was heading straight for hell.

In those tense moments before battle, he found himself reading a book of prayers when Romans 10:9 caught his eye: "It said: 'If you confess with your mouth that Jesus is Lord and believe in your heart that God raised Him from the dead, you will be saved.'

"I thought it was some kind of loophole in the Bible," he says, as if he'd found the back door into heaven left open by accident. But he decided to "take God at His word. And a week later, friends were asking me why I was so different."

Murphy knew what the difference was—the same difference he's continuing to make today in the lives of his soldiers in Iraq. After many years as an infantryman, Major Murphy is now regimental chaplain for the 325th, overseeing a handful of others responsible for ministering to the needs of the men in their units.

"We're Christian ministers," he says, pointedly, of the five chaplains who serve in his regiment. "We make the difference between souls going to hell and souls going to heaven." For soldiers facing mortality on a daily basis, Murphy knows the unvarnished message of the Scripture is critical to their lives, their duties, their futures. "A lot of Christians think chaplains have to water down their faith to fit in. It's just not so."

Yet they realize this is a line they must walk with care. Though their own beliefs are evangelical, Murphy says they do their best to help soldiers of other faiths find someone who can help them worship in their faith tradition. "I don't view this as a compromise of my faith; rather, it's part of my role as a Christian minister."

As is prayer. *His* prayer. His *men's* prayers. And the prayers of the church, standing guard in the homeland.

"We could tell a difference when the people back home were praying for us and when they weren't. It was like night and day," the Pennsylvania native says. He seemed to feel it most especially during July and August when the war was officially ebbing but reports of death were continuing. That's when "conditions were the worst and morale was the lowest. When people started praying for us again toward the end of August, that's when things started turning around."

So Murphy and his men remain on duty. Serving. Praying. Making a difference every day in the hearts of American soldiers and in the future of Iraq.

"We're Christian ministers. We make the difference between souls going to hell and souls going to heaven."

Major Jim Murphy

Steel Base Memorial Chapel's white walls shine clean and spotless in the dusty environment it's surrounded by at BIAP. The solid structure is a welcome change from canvas tents that formerly served as the chapel. This is the first service in the newly built chapel—dedicated to the memory of fellow soldiers who have died.

# GOD'S MAN AMONG MEN

Chaplain (Captain) Eddie Cook deployed with his unit to Kuwait on February 14, 2003—Valentine's Day. Over the following weeks, he shared the gospel with every one of his men, numbering in the "several hundreds." (Security specifications do not allow exact numbers of units and battalions to be published.)

Eighty-six of them accepted Christ.

For nine days, during a training mission to Falaka Island, Cook baptized all eighty-six. He stood waist-deep in the waters of the Persian Gulf, his smile doing nothing to hide his excitement as the men lined up like dominos along shore, waiting to be baptized.

"It was an awesome time in the Lord," Cook remembers. "As I stood in the surf, seeing the crowd and the line, I could imagine how John the Baptist felt"—and could hardly underestimate the importance, the timing, the gravity of the moment. For what none of them knew then—that their parachute assault mission on a Baghdad airfield would be called off—was that they were about to take part in one of the first significant battles of the war.

Paratroopers . . . in a ground assault convoy.

Photograph courtesy of Cook family

# The First Battle: Al Samawah

Crossing the border of Kuwait into Iraq, the combat team that Cook accompanied made their cautious approach into the city of Al Samawah. The walk was hot and sweltering—especially for March—the heat wave simply adding to their already simmering nerves.

Several miles away from their objective, the dull thud of their own boots and the occasional snap of a twig were the only sounds heard as they marched through groves of palm trees, silhouetted in the twilight of the evening.

Cook lowered his night vision goggles for a better look.

Stunned at what he saw, his breath caught in his throat.

It was tracer fire, shooting straight toward them, oddly looking much like the Fourth of July fireworks he remembered from his boyhood days in Hickory, North Carolina. Only, aiming to kill.

Realizing what was ahead, he quickly prayed for God's protection over the men. "We took mortar fire several times, some landing within fifteen feet of the soldiers, without getting hurt," Cook remembers. "This can only be God."

All that day and for the next two weeks, the troops pushed the Iraqi army back, preventing them from advancing on U.S. positions. Like clockwork, Cook was always there to pray for the men before their combat teams headed out for another mission. He moved alongside them as they maneuvered into position—the chaplain, on the prowl with his men, praying in the line of fire.

It's not unlike him to be in the thick of things. According to Geneva Convention guidelines, Cook (like all chaplains) is not allowed to carry a weapon. But that doesn't prevent him from getting shot at. One afternoon, on his way to a workout in another building where the men had built a makeshift gym, he was walking across the compound when someone handed him his mail, which included a letter from his wife. Anxious to read it, he headed back to his room and, as he was looking through the letter, heard three large explosions. An RPG attack. Running out with the other soldiers to investigate, he saw that one of the incoming rounds had squarely hit the weight bench where he would have been sitting had he not been delayed.

Another time, sitting in the back of a cargo jeep, his group of soldiers began taking fire from a man with a pistol. "That didn't bother me so much, but when we started chasing him, men started shooting at us from the rooftops," Cook recalls. It was a setup, and not being able to see where the shots were coming from created a tense, helpless feeling. After the man brandishing the pistol was killed and loaded onto the truck, the crowd of locals closed in around them. "It felt like the streets of Mogadishu from *Blackhawk Down*," Cook says. "We pushed them away and made our way through the narrow alleys to the main road, which was our first time traveling in that direction. God, again, was with us and saw us out."

> **"We took mortar fire several times, some landing within fifteen feet of the soldiers, without getting hurt. This can only be God."** Chaplain Cook

Just as He did here, in Al Samawah.

These first clashes of all-out warfare caused several casualties in Cook's unit over the course of the next few days. But no deaths. As the injured came into the battalion aid station where doctor and medics waited, Cook prayed with the fallen, escorting them to the field ambulance or helicopter for evacuation.

"I always help carry the stretcher or walk beside my soldier to load him up," Cook explains. Each time he saw another helicopter lift off with an injured soldier in tow, he prayed it would be "the last time I have to see another one of my men evacuated."

## A Soldier's Chaplain

Cook always wanted to be a soldier though he didn't always plan to be a chaplain. His father was Army—82nd Airborne during the Korean War era. It was something Cook idolized as a child.

After graduating from North Carolina State University in 1992 with a double major in economics and business management, he went straight to Fort Bragg as an infantry officer on a ROTC officer's commission.

Already a Christian, saved at a young age, it wasn't until he was an infantry platoon leader that he felt God calling him into the ministry.

As part of the 82nd's A Company, 1st Battalion, 505 Parachute Infantry Regiment, Cook noticed how rarely their chaplain came to visit them for services while they were out in the field . . . and never on their deployments to Panama and Germany.

"My men would ask me if there would be church services, so we would meet together and I would read Scripture and pray," Cook says. "God showed me He was calling me to stand in the gap and take His Word to soldiers."

Under the mentorship of another chaplain, Cook left the Army in 1997 to attend Southeastern Baptist Theological Seminary in Wake Forest, North Carolina, and served as a missionary in North Africa. There he met his wife, also serving. He returned as a chaplain in 2002, endorsed by the Assemblies of God in Springfield, Missouri.

> **" My men would ask me if there would be church services, so we would meet together and I would read Scripture and pray. God showed me that He was calling me to stand in the gap and take His Word to soldiers."**
>
> **Chaplain Cook**

## Among Friends

Chaplains share a special bond. Chaplain Cook visits the tent of a fellow chaplain on base.

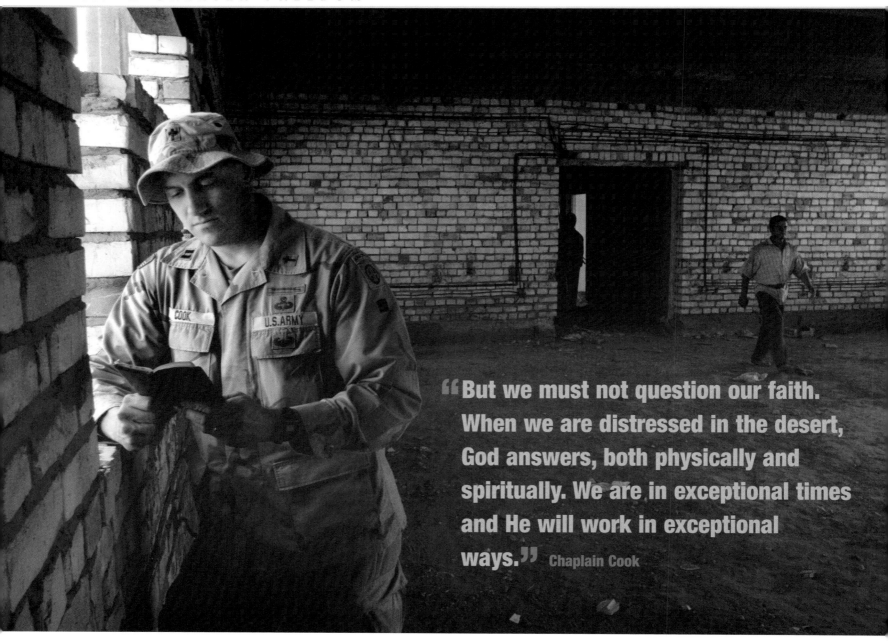

"But we must not question our faith. When we are distressed in the desert, God answers, both physically and spiritually. We are in exceptional times and He will work in exceptional ways." Chaplain Cook

It's clear the lives and the souls of his men mean a great deal to Chaplain Cook, now thirty-three. He can tell you many stories of how God is working in their midst:

There's SPC Nicholas Puetz, who was saved and baptized with the others on Falaka Island, now eagerly attending Bible study and chapel services.

There's CPT Justin Hufnaegel, who sought Cook's counsel about becoming a stronger spiritual leader for his family.

Then there's SPC Bradley Brown, whom Cook met when Brown approached him back in Fayetteville about finding a church for his family. The chaplain invited him to chapel on the base, which they started attending. Brown began attending Cook's Bible study after deployment. With a passion.

"One night at a Bible study, I encouraged everyone to take some New Testaments and give them out while sharing the Roman Road to salvation," Cook remembers. "Bradley immediately left with a Bible and witnessed to the first person he came to. He ran back in so excited and said, 'I gotta get some more Bibles!' That's the kind of excitement God wants us all to have, with a heart for evangelism."

That was in March.

Tragedy struck in August.

Brown was leaving his compound on a truck with several other soldiers when an improvised explosive device (IED) blew up, severely injuring his eyes and ears, leaving him with multiple shrapnel wounds. Cook immediately hurried to the forward support medical station where the men were taken, going to each gurney, praying with the men one by one.

He didn't recognize Brown at first, his face distorted by his own blood.

"Is that you, Chaplain?" a familiar voice asked.

Cook looked again. Brown did his best to sit up. Realizing it was his friend, Cook hugged him, comforted him, prayed with him. And this time, while accompanying "yet another stretcher to the helicopter dust off," Cook knew he was sending one home with Good News from the front lines—how God can spare a man's life in combat, how Christ can change a man's heart in crisis.

"Bradley's returned to the States and is recovering," Cook happily reports, "attending chapel and witnessing how God spared his life. He is a true friend and encouragement."

Truly, the friendship goes both ways.

## The Visible Power of Prayer

More than anything else during his time in Iraq, Cook says God has taught him the power of prayer.

Shortly before the war, the battalion moved to the Kuwait desert, shooting at ranges. Suddenly, a huge windstorm hit the men full force, causing them to hunker down under their ponchos, trying desperately to wait out the storm.

Cook felt the voice of God telling him to pray for the wind to calm, and other soldiers around him were asking as well. He did—but silently, to himself. Almost immediately, the shrill eighty-miles-per-hour wind throttled down to a breeze.

"I praised God for it, but I felt Him ask me why I hadn't prayed out loud so that all could see Him work," Cook recalls. "I remembered Christ and His rebuking of the storm. But I felt like that was of biblical proportions, and I was pretty skeptical of doing that myself in front of everyone.

"But we must not question our faith. When we are distressed in the desert, God answers, both physically and spiritually," says Cook. "God instilled in me we are in exceptional times, and He will work in exceptional ways."

So God gave Cook another chance.

After leaving the desert, the men returned to the base camp, where they lived in large fifty-man tents. Late one evening as the men slept, they woke to the sounds of metal poles snapping, thrashing about the heads of their cots. Lights crashed down around them. The center poles wobbled as the men rushed to hold them down.

Another windstorm.

Over the whooshing sound of the wind and the flapping of the tent now threatening to break, someone yelled out, "Chaplain, pray for us!"

Cook's thoughts flashed back to the desert—his silent prayer, his halfway fear of faith. Stepping away from the pole he was holding down, he stood to his feet in the middle of the tent and called upon the name of Jesus to calm the wind, to save them.

And then . . . it was quiet. The tremendous gusts knocking even large soldiers to the ground were gone. In its place, a small breeze still blew.

The storm stopped.

> **"God honored my prayer as I was faithful to His Word, as I was obeying and glorifying Him. He made His name real to all those who witnessed this. We continue to witness the power of God working daily here at war. As God shows His faithfulness, He draws men to salvation."** Chaplain Cook

"The men all looked at me in amazement. And I think I looked pretty amazed, too," Cook says, smiling. "I remembered the fig tree [from Jesus' encounter with Nathanael in John 1:50]. 'Have faith in God. This you will do and greater things than this will you do.'

"God honored my prayer as I was faithful to His Word, as I was obeying and glorifying Him. He made His name real to all those who witnessed this. We continue to witness the power of God working daily here at war. As God shows His faithfulness, He draws men to salvation."

> **"I pray a lot. You can't turn to the guys next to you and talk to them about it—what you did, what you saw—because it was their friend too."**
>
> **SPC Brent Gothier**

# SAYING GOOD-BYE

It's never easy when you lose a man. It's even tougher when you lose two: one to severe injuries, one to death.

Specialist Brent Gothier, twenty-four, is a medic with the 3rd Battalion, 325th, from Hartington, Nebraska. His job is tough. When he performs his duty, he's not working on strangers; he's trying to save the life of a buddy.

This was the case the day their squad was hit by a volley of rocket propelled grenades (RPGs). A group of their men were guarding a weapons turn-in site when a van stopped directly across the street. As a crowd of Iraqis formed around the van, three men pumped RPGs into the American soldiers.

"There were still some shots being fired when we rolled into the scene," Gothier remembers. He went to work helping one of the two young soldiers who was down on the ground.

One was mortally wounded in the head.

The other young soldier was hit in the hand and legs. "He had serious femoral bleeds in both of his legs, and his left hand had been amputated by the force of the blast. He stopped breathing on us at one point, so we performed rescue breathing. It was hard because just four or five hours earlier, I'd been eating MREs with him."

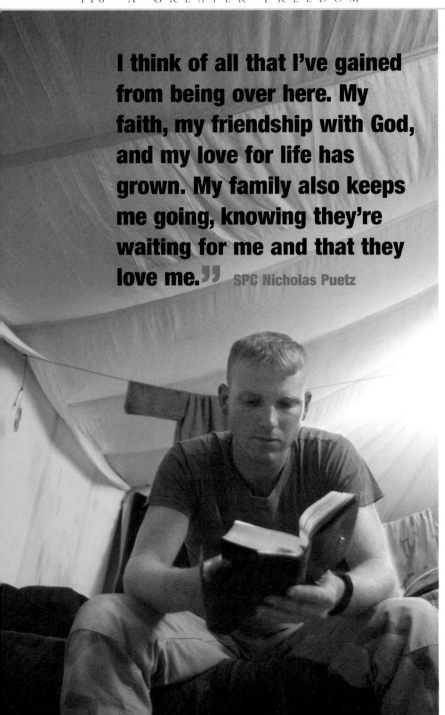

I think of all that I've gained from being over here. My faith, my friendship with God, and my love for life has grown. My family also keeps me going, knowing they're waiting for me and that they love me." SPC Nicholas Puetz

Chaplain Cook points to this RPG attack as one of the most gut-wrenching things he's seen during the war. He remembers praying over the injured soldier, who wouldn't wake up until several weeks later—at Walter Reed Medical Center—without legs and a left hand.

Cook also remembers the other soldier . . . who died in his arms.

"I held him and prayed over him, whispering the Twenty-third Psalm in the one ear he had left, comforting him with the words of eternal life," Cook says. He admits this soldier's death, the first for the battalion, stirred many emotions.

"I was infuriated at the enemy and hurt by the loss of one of my men God trusted me to shepherd. We had fought from Kuwait to Baghdad without losing a man. And now . . . this.

"God taught me it wasn't due to a breach in righteousness, but the consequence of war. As death is the consequence of sin, so it is in war."

It's a consequence Gothier must also deal with.

"I pray a lot," he says, when asked how he copes, seeing his buddies injured, or worse. "I'm big on prayer. You can't turn to the guys next to you and talk to them about it—what you did, what you saw—because it was their friend too."

While Gothier says his faith has "definitely grown during this time," it's certainly been challenged since deployment began. "There's a lot of anger toward the things that have happened, and I'm dealing with stuff as it comes," he says, his voice low, his words spoken slowly, thoughtfully. "I'm not sure what the purpose is [of seeing soldiers die]. But I'm staying strong in my faith."

# Blackhawk Down

SPC Nicholas Puetz, from Phoenix, Arizona, is also a medic with the 3rd Battalion, 2nd Brigade combat team. Though he grew up in a Christian family, he says it wasn't until he got to Kuwait and started attending the chapel services that things "started to click and make sense." He accepted Christ there—one of the first to be baptized at Falaka Island.

Many miles and memories later, he found himself flying at night in a group of Blackhawk helicopters in Iraq, when the helicopter in front of them suddenly went down.

"One guy was thrown out and the helicopter rolled over him," Puetz says, remembering. "When we got there, it was on fire. They put out the fire and dragged him away. We had six or seven medics on the scene, but he was pretty bad off. That's probably the worst thing I've seen."

Asked whether the soldier lived, he silently shakes his head.

For the twenty-four-year-old Puetz, it is his faith alone that helps him deal with situations like these, with fighting in a war. "It's hard to explain, but you think of all the things that could go wrong, and you just know God is watching over us. I think of all I've gained from being over here. My faith, my friendship with God, and my love for life has grown. My family also keeps me going, knowing they're waiting for me and that they love me."

# STAYING THE COURSE

**Y**ou don't have to look very far to get a good idea of what Baghdad is like today, almost a year since major combat operations were officially declared over. Bombed-out, burned, and looted buildings still line the neighborhoods. Thick, white chalky dust coats everything, sticking in the back of your throat and sneaking under your fingernails. To an unknowing observer, this might look like a godless place.

But for others, Baghdad is a symbol of what God can and will do for the people of Iraq. It is this faith that gives hope to the troops—hope that they'll eventually head safely home and hope that they are leaving behind something of lasting importance: a free and liberated Iraq.

There are no foxholes for hiding in this city of five million people. Ask any soldier and they'll quickly tell you: there's no defined front line for the war they're still fighting. Instead, there are mortar attacks to listen for, IEDs to avoid, and a chance the car stopped in front of you is an ambush. Body armor is a common part of the uniform here.

Given the situation, many acknowledge that the questions of "why" have frequently entered their minds. Why are we here? Why are we doing this? Why is this worth risking my life and being separated for months on end from my children, my family?

This has proven for many a high-tech testing ground for the "whys" of life. The "whys" of death. Of war. Of peace. Of everything.

## Keeping Watch

He keeps his weapon ready, his eye keen, watching out for potential trouble. He's not just looking out for himself, for his fellow soldiers traveling with him. He's watching out for the little Iraqi girl waving from the car, for her parents, for her family. It's why she waves. She knows the initial difference "the Americans" have made. She will later see the long-term effect.

To an unknowing observer, this might look like a godless place. But for others, Baghdad has become a symbol of what God can and will do for the people of Iraq.

**Staff Sergeant Doug Hopkins of Greensboro, North Carolina, with the 422nd Civil Affairs Division, helps a local Iraqi on the side of the road in Baghdad.**

## Coping

'You really do have to separate from what you see here," said Lieutenant Hope Simmons of Tampa, Florida, about her work
BN SINA Hospital located in what's called "the Green Zone" of Baghdad. The hospital was at one time used as Saddam
Hussein's personal hospital for himself, his family, and his close supporters. "Initially death was the hardest thing to deal
with, but now it's dealing with the buddy of the one who died. Sometimes it's really hard for them to understand why they'
still standing and their buddy isn't." Simmons, twenty-five, is a member of New Life Christian Center who has been in Iraq
since March. She hopes to attend medical school when she goes home. "I've really been trying to make more of an effort to

Joseph Larrew, part of the 372nd Mobile Public Affairs Detachment, uses his downtime to review Scripture, which he says helps keep his faith strong.

# A BETTER PLACE

"As a sniper, my job is to kill people," says Sergeant James Crowell, scout sniper with the 3rd Battalion. "That's the coldhearted reality of it."

He's been with his current reconnaissance platoon, part of Bravo Company, since late 2002, and says it's the closest group of friends he's ever had. He joined the Army in the summer of 2000, following in the footsteps of his father, a lieutenant colonel who served as a captain in Desert Storm.

Crowell was one of those eighty-six soldiers baptized by Chaplain Cook in the waters of the Persian Gulf off Falaka Island. He grew up in church and attended Cumberland United Methodist near his base in Fayetteville, North Carolina, before deployment. But it took an impending war for him to finally understand what it meant to have a relationship with God.

He's needed it every minute of every day since.

**"It's a comforting feeling to know that the man upstairs, no matter what happens and how crazy things get, I know He'll be here to give me the guidance to get the job done and to stay safe."**

**Sgt. James Crowell**

"Getting ready to head into war, it really comes down to a fear of the unknown. I remember calling my mom a couple of days before the war started and breaking down in tears. I was more scared about losing one of my buddies and not coming back with one of them.

"It's a comforting feeling to know that the man upstairs, no matter what happens and how crazy things get, I know He'll be here to give me the guidance to get the job done and to stay safe," Crowell says. "I love God and I trust Him every day like I'm not going to live the next. I know He has His own special plan for me.

"I don't want to necessarily go in and kill people, but if that's what my job entails, I'll do it, y'know . . . to make the world a better place."

Only twenty-two, Crowell has seen a lot of things that most others his age never will. He doesn't want to grow hard at the death and destruction he's witnessed. He tries not to retain too much of what he sees. It's important to him to maintain his sense of humanity.

But some things are just too hard to forget . . . like Al Samawah.

It started out just like any other day at war for a scout. He positioned himself along with a few others from his unit on the roof of a train station, watching over a platoon of soldiers moving from hut to hut within a village, looking for an Iraqi general. The general, knowing U.S. forces were beginning to pinch, had lost his weapon and uniform and was trying to blend in with the locals.

Then came fresh orders from the platoon leader—for Crowell to go check the other side from his rooftop post. After getting into position, he leaned forward on his elbow, peering through his scope. Three clicks away (one click equals one kilometer)—still beyond the eighteen-hundred-meter range of his sniper rifle—he could see an ambulance coming down the road, lights flashing.

Crowell watched as the vehicle came to a stop. Three men got out.

Looking around, they disappeared behind a nearby hill.

"At the same time, about one click away, Alpha Company was moving toward an area they had to search, and they started taking mortar rounds and mortar fire," he remembers. Crowell saw the white plumes of smoke coming up over the hill—the hill he just saw the three Iraqis walk behind.

He knew at once it was a mortar position. They were shooting at Americans.

"I had two forward observers up there [on the roof with him] and two terminal attack controllers that control aircraft and, uh . . . we went to work pretty much marking targets," he says.

*Marking targets.* Code words for gunning down enemies.

"That went on ten or fifteen minutes, taking those guys out, and I didn't really let it get to me. These guys were trying to kill my friends, my family. I was thinking, *I gotta stop them.*"

During the heat of these exchanges, the Kiowa helicopter gun ships that had been called in flew over the edge of the city. As they came closer, thirty Feyadeen commandos appeared, firing what seemed to be an enormous amount of guns and rocket launchers. As the helicopters returned fire with rockets and hellfire missiles, killing a couple of the elite Iraqi special forces, Crowell watched through the scope of his rifle with shock and disbelief.

"The Feyadeen started going to the houses there, bringing out old men and women and children and forcing them to stand in a circle around them," Crowell says.

The frightened civilians stood vulnerable and defenseless, at the battle's most violent point. Those desperately trying to run back into their homes and away from the line of fire were shot and killed instantly. The Feyadeen now aimed their weapons not toward the oncoming enemy but at their very own countrymen.

This is war at its worst.

"Why were those guys taking innocent people and doing that to them?" Crowell asks. "Women and children and old men. People who are defenseless, just trying to live a life. You kind of stow something like that in a deep, dark corner of your heart and hope you never have to see that again."

From what he does choose to remember of this war, Crowell says it's the Iraqi children who stand out most in his mind—smiling, waving peace signs, so excited when a soldier says a simple hello. But he also sees them selling cigarettes and anything else they can offer in order to help feed their families, "playing on streets filled with defecation."

"It's made me promise myself that I will stay and do this job no matter how long it takes to make the world a better place.

"There are a lot of bad people out there, and they need to be dealt with. I don't want my kids worrying about being bombed on a school bus when they go to school. I don't want my kids to have to live like this."

As part of a reconnaissance platoon, Crowell sees a side of the Iraqi people that a lot of the infantry and other soldiers don't get to see. Typically, his unit relies on the Iraqis themselves to help them carry out their missions, asking permission of Iraqi families to use their houses as observation points. More often than not, they say yes.

"Aside from what the public wants to think and what the media wants them to know, not all Iraqis are bad. Not all Arabs are bad," Crowell says. "With these recon missions I was on, I actually got to see that. I got to see these people are just like me, just like my mom and dad. They've got kids going to school, and they're trying to make a life. If you see that, you know there's hope out there.

"Aside from the fragile situation that Iraq is in right now, there are a lot of people out there who really believe they can see the light at the end of this very dark tunnel that Saddam Hussein has put them in. I'm just very thankful I had the opportunity to experience that because I can go back now and I can tell my kids and everybody else back home, 'You may think one thing, but it's totally different. It's not that way.'"

The world is becoming a better place.

> **"I love God and I trust Him every day like I'm not going to live the next. I know He has his own special plan for me."**
>
> **Sergeant Crowell**

"Aside from what the public wants to think and what the media wants them to know, not all Iraqis are bad. Not all Arabs are bad. With these recon missions I was on, I actually got to see that. I got to see these people are just like me, just like my mom and dad. They've got kids going to school, and they're trying to make a life. If you see that, you know there's hope out there. Aside from the fragile situation that Iraq is in right now, there are a lot of people out there who really believe they can see the light at the end of this very dark tunnel that Saddam Hussein has put them in." **Sergeant Crowell**

## Building a New Iraq

Iraqis and Americans are working together to bring new life to an old country. Schools, hospitals, churches, and new roads are slowly appearing in place of the rubble.

# THE ARMS OF CHRIST

The toughest moment 1st Lieutenant Brett Bailey has experienced since he's been in Iraq had absolutely nothing to do with a mission, an attack, or an injury to a fellow soldier.

It had everything to do with a single phone call.

Bailey had waited almost four hours in line, anxious to talk to his wife of two years for the first time since his deployment two weeks before—but never expecting to hear this kind of news. The last time he'd seen her, she excitedly told him he was going to be a father. Knowing he couldn't be there to see her through her pregnancy had dampened the happy news with a twinge of pain. Nothing like this.

"I think I lost the baby," she said.

She had suffered a miscarriage.

"That was the toughest time for me and her—probably the time where our faith grew the most because for the first time since I've known her, I really could not help her at all," he says. "I had to completely turn her protection over to God.

"I wanted to be there to help her through it, protect her, just to give her a hug. And I really had to rely on Christ to give her that hug for me, to provide everything."

Bailey, a member of First Assembly of God in Fayetteville, North Carolina, says while the separation through such a difficult time is extremely hard, he and his wife have both grown in their faith and are seeing God work through their lives and their marriage to make it stronger.

"We know everything happens for a reason, though we don't always see it; but even already, God has healed a lot of our wounds," he says, pointing out his wife has ministered to other women who have experienced the same tragedy. "It's definitely not a good thing, but God can turn it around for good, even in the worst of situations."

Fair-haired and blue-eyed, Bailey's gentle smile and easygoing personality more closely resemble the typical all-American boy next door than the scout platoon leader that he is. A twenty-five-year-old native of Brookeville,

Pennsylvania, he and his wife are graduates of Evangel College in Springfield, Missouri, where he received his officer's commission through ROTC in 2001.

Just as he's seen God work in his marriage and the loss of a child, he's also seen God at work in the midst of war, bringing freedom to the Iraqi people and in the very lives of the soldiers he's responsible for.

> **"That was the toughest time for me and her—probably the time where our faith grew the most because for the first time since I've known her, I really could not help her at all. I had to completely turn her protection over to God."**
>
> **Lt. Brett Bailey**

"When you think about Army guys, especially guys in the airborne-infantry, they're the risk-takers. They feel invincible many times," Bailey explains. "But war puts a new perspective on life. They don't take it for granted as much anymore. When that happens, they start thinking about how life can be fragile and they're not guaranteed the next day."

He's seen many of the men make first-time commitments to Christ, commitments that seem to be deep, the changes within their lives real—not a "battlefield conversion; it's really sticking." A Bible study was formed because of the large numbers of new believers. More than thirty men attend, meeting to discuss everything from the basics of Christianity to tougher issues like whether it's scriptural to pray against your enemy.

Bailey knows why these soldiers make such good Christians.

"They know what it is to serve. They know what it is to have something bigger and more important than yourself," he says. "They've given their lives to defend their country, to bring earthly freedom to people.

"The greatest freedom you can give people is, first and foremost, freedom from sin. And second, freedom from oppression, from tyranny.

"Soldiers who are Christians are doing both."

**"They know what it is to serve. They know what it is to have something bigger and more important than yourself. They've given their lives to defend their country, to bring earthly freedom to people. The greatest freedom you can give people is, first and foremost, freedom from sin. And second, freedom from oppression, from tyranny. Soldiers who are Christians are doing both."** Lieutenant Bailey

## My Soldiers and My God

Timothy McFayden is one of those real-life soldier Christians, who's been a regular part of
Bailey's Bible study back when there were only
eight men coming, before they had to move to
a bigger room to accommodate everybody.

A platoon sergeant with the 3rd Battalion,
McFayden now has fifteen years in the Army
dating back to Desert Storm. This time is
harder, though, now that he has a family waiting on him to come home.

"None of us thought we'd be here this
long," he says, sitting in his room, his back
propped up against a locker door revealing
several pictures of his children and family. "We
thought six months max and we'd be home."

A member of Strickland Bridge Road Church
of God in Fayetteville, the sergeant says it's his
men and his God who keep him going. As a
leader of a thirty-eight man platoon, it's his
responsibility to make sure each one of them
is OK, both physically and emotionally. It's his
job to help them see they're making a difference though their current position south of the
city takes them out of direct contact with the
neighborhoods of Baghdad.

It hasn't been easy, like the day one of his men was injured when someone threw a homemade bomb into their company from an overpass, basically a paint can loaded with screws. He acknowledges that their company and battalion haven't had as many injuries and deaths as others. He credits it all to prayer and to God.

"Faith is definitely important. My faith gives me peace."

# "Faith is definitely important. My faith gives me peace."

Sgt. Timothy McFayden

"They surrendered the hospital and we had the city. God went before us and the city was taken without the culminating battle. All of us knew the power of God that night." Chaplain Eddie Cook

# GOD'S PROTECTION

It was the beginning of March, still in the earliest phase of the war, and the outcome for this 3rd Battalion night mission didn't look good. Several hundred Feyadeen soldiers had taken over a hospital in Al Samawah, using patients as shields.

The 3rd Battalion's orders were simple: take the hospital. Their only course of action was a planned battalion assault, starting at the ground floor and working their way up through the building—all eleven floors.

For several days leading up to the mission, scouts reported seeing buses filled with civilians driven by the Feyadeen, preparing to lock down into battle positions. The disadvantage to the U.S. troops was great, having no knowledge of the hospital's floor plan and knowing that whatever path they took, the Feyadeen would see them coming.

Everyone knew where this was heading: it would be a bloodbath. A great number of people were about to die.

The day arrived, the men pumped and prepared for battle. Almost all attended the chapel service that Chaplain Cook held—some wearing war paint on their faces (usually not used in the desert), some whose eyes showed fear, others alive with intense excitement, but as Cook says, "all looking to their God." He prayed with each company for God to spare the men and give victory over the enemy, letting righteousness prevail.

Finally, the hour was at hand.

## "Thank You, Jesus!"

The battalion began a unified advance toward the hospital, adding combat power as they approached.

Then suddenly, at the last minute, with only a few hundred meters separating them from their objective, the mission was called off.

The Feyadeen surrendered.

"They surrendered the hospital, and we had the city," Cook says, smiling at the memory. "God went before us, and the city was taken without the culminating battle. All of us knew the power of God that night."

"It was a sigh of relief when that happened," Sergeant Crowell admits. "It just looked like a bad plan, and though we were ready to do it, it felt like we were chasing the phantom menace."

"Just looking at the mission we had to do, it was going to be very ugly," says Sergeant McFayden. "It would have forced our guys to make the decision between second-guessing themselves when they got in there or just shooting when they hit the door. As we were stepping off for the mission and we got word it was canceled, I was like 'Thank You, Jesus!'"

Not everyone was as relieved. Several of the men who were psyched for battle approached Cook, very angry. "This is your fault," they told the chaplain. "We wanted to go! We were ready to fight and you prayed to your God!"

McFayden offers his perspective: "Up to that point, we'd always had the upper hand, but in a situation like that, we weren't going to have the upper hand." You can say what you want, but "God was looking out for us."

And it wasn't the first time. Nor the last. Through the course of the war, Brett Bailey says they've definitely seen God's protection.

"He's definitely always been in control," Bailey says. "You can look at all of the things we never saw happen—

> **"At no point did I feel God left me, but I knew I had left Him."**
> Sean Dickson

the IEDs we drove past that didn't explode, the sixty-millimeter mortars that landed ten meters away and didn't blow up. We've had multiple times where guys have stepped around a corner within twenty-five feet of us and opened up with a full magazine and an A-K, and nobody gets hit."

He chalks some of it up to his observation that the Iraqis typically "aren't good shots." But at the same time, "there are too many coincidences to be coincidences."

This can only be God.

## Fenced In

God's protection has been seen not only on a battalion level but on an individual level as well.

Sean Dickson, a twenty-five-year-old sniper from Birmingham, Alabama, never had strong ties to church growing up and found himself struggling as a teenager. Fresh out of high school, he spent his time partying, his life headed nowhere . . . until a friend of his invited him to church. Dickson started attending Jubilee Ministries Fellowship with him in Birmingham and says that's where he accepted Christ for the first time in his life. "Everything was suddenly bearable," he recalls.

"I now walk around knowing I'm not in charge here. I make decisions along the way, but for the most part, God is in charge of me. That's why I'm here."

He admits, though, his faith took a backseat to combat when his unit first entered Iraq. "I was so focused on killing that, for probably our entire country crossing, I forgot to pray." Understandable. It isn't hard to have that kind

of focus as a soldier. Your previous training, combined with the knowledge that someone is trying to kill you, just sort of kicks in, overriding all other thoughts. "At no point did I feel God left me, but I knew I had left Him."

So one evening before a big mission, he decided to attend the regular chapel service Chaplain Cook held on Saturday evenings.

And a mere six hours later, he was in the firefight of his life.

**"I now walk around knowing I'm not in charge here. I make decisions along the way, but for the most part, God is in charge of me."** Sean Dickson

In the early morning hours, still cloaked by darkness, he and three other soldiers from his group had been dropped off for their mission. As typical for their jobs, they were by themselves, miles away from any backup. Crouched on top of a roof, they listened to the droning sound of the Muslim call to prayer, echoing off the walls of the buildings around them.

As the last note sounded, shots rang out. Dickson could feel the bullets whiz past his head.

He and his unit were under attack, taking fire from three houses just across the street from their position. In all directions.

Seeing the flashes of bullets below them, the men had no choice but to jump off the roof in order to take cover. While the other three soldiers took position behind a wall, Dickson ran up to an iron gate and positioned his rifle on top, shooting back at the attackers.

"I never saw or heard a single bullet come by me, but I heard this overwhelming voice telling me to move, that this wasn't a safe place and I had to move," Dickson says.

He did, finding a new position behind a wall. The firefight raged on for twenty minutes more until reinforcements were called in. After the battle, the men walked back to the wall where it all began and saw the entire area was riddled with bullet holes.

Yet no one got hit.

Dickson looked at the gate he'd initially hidden behind, the position where he sensed God warning him of imminent danger. "All around the gate were bullet holes, but right where my chest had leaned up against it were thirteen dents," he says. "This gate in no way should have stopped a single bullet, not 762s."

And still on his chestplate, where it had been ever since leaving Kuwait, was his copy of Psalm 91, an ancient prayer for God's protection.

Dickson has no doubt God was looking out for him. "I'm definitely not in charge here," Dickson says emphatically. "I put myself in a place to die, but God pulled me out of it."

## Near Misses

Daniel Galloway is a first lieutenant infantry platoon leader with the battalion. Now thirty-one, he joined the Army in 1991, meeting his future wife in the process. Today, Galloway is in Baghdad; his wife is in Ramadi, two hours away. Their two children (currently ten and two) are back home with grandparents in St. Louis.

Truly, the last couple of years haven't been easy on the family.

Though he admits he's in the most trying situation of his life—missing his wife, missing his kids—he says his faith has definitely grown because he's seen how God has isolated their battalion from harm.

There have been numerous close calls. Being in a forward-most unit, he's stood directly in front of the bad guys. He's seen the mortar rounds come in. He's felt the RPGs land ten meters in front of him.

"Obviously, the Lord is looking out for us over here," Galloway says, who last attended Faith Outreach near Fort Campbell, Kentucky, before transferring to the 82nd in Fayetteville shortly before shipping out. "He's definitely got an overall plan, a plan that needs to be accomplished, and He needs guys to do it."

The most recent near miss was a hand grenade thrown at one of his platoon's trucks, landing five meters from the vehicle.

"As usual, it was close, and not even a scratch," Galloway says, shaking his head in grateful awe.

Not all of the soldiers see it as God's protection. One of Galloway's men is an atheist. When an RPG hit the front of

**"Obviously, the Lord is looking out for us over here. He's definitely got an overall plan, a plan that needs to be accomplished, and He needs guys to do it."** Lt. Daniel Galloway

the truck he was driving, this soldier walked away with only a minor injury. Galloway told him he thought angels were watching out for him. But the soldier dismissed it, saying the Iraqi wasn't trained properly, that it was a bad shot.

"He gave 101 different ways to put a secular spin on it. But I still hold to the belief that the Lord will use that later on in this guy's life," Galloway says. "He'll come to a crossroads, and he's going to think back about almost dying on a particular day and how he walked away with a scratch."

The protection, the safety, and the minimal casualties they've experienced—compared to what could have been—is not by accident, many of the men say.

"I think it's a direct result of all the prayers going on back home," says Lieutenant Bailey. "I'm anxious to hear all of the stories about God waking someone up in the middle of the night and saying, 'Hey, you need to pray for them.'"

**The sword-bearing right hands of Saddam Hussein are now only reminders of the former dictator's rule.**

In a Baghdad neighborhood, tank commander SFC John Bernard from Chandler, Arizona, rides topside while on tank patrol with others from the 1st Armored Division, 1st Battalion, Alpha Company.

PFC Nickolas Abramovitz from Tampa, Florida, is a tank driver for the 1st Armored Division, 1st Battalion, Alpha Company.

**"God is our refuge and strength, a helper who is always found in times of trouble."** Psalm 46:1

## One Soldier's Faith

Believing in Christ means holding a Christian worldview. This biblical perspective comes with its own way of responding to your environment, to all the situations around you. You can profess to believe whatever you will, but the beliefs you truly hold in your heart will find themselves lived out through your convictions, your morals, your actions, your attitudes. You can't separate one from the other.

If you're a soldier, then, your faith has a huge impact on how you handle your duty, your response to war, and your ability to hope in things eternal when all around you seems lost and insurmountable. It's a sense of freedom that only comes from a relationship with Jesus Christ.

David Elsen knows this. He is a captain in military intelligence for the 3-325th. A graduate of Wheaton College near Chicago, Illinois, Elsen says while the war has, to a certain extent, been a test of faith for him, he hasn't felt any doubt that he's where he's supposed to be.

"I've had to deal with fear from time to time," he admits, "but I feel like I'm where I need to be, and I'm doing what I'm supposed to be doing, and it's going to be all right. The Lord's going to take care of me one way or the other. He's going to take care of my family.

"I'm here for a purpose. *We're* here for a purpose . . . and I've felt that the whole time.

"If I didn't have my faith, I don't know how I would function," he says. "I had peace going into war, not knowing what was in front of us because ultimately I know where I'm headed. I gave my life to Christ at an early age and I'm rock-solid confident that if something happens to me, I'm going to spend eternity with Him, so I'm not worried.

**"If I didn't have my faith, I don't know how I would function. I had peace going into war, not knowing what was in front of us because ultimately I know where I'm headed."**

**Captain David Elsen**

"My worry, if anything, is my family." Elsen has a three-month-old son back home he's never seen. "I don't want to get killed and leave them behind because of the pain it would cause them. For me personally, I don't really fear, but if I didn't have that faith, it would be a pretty uncertain thing not knowing from day to day if your life is going to be asked of you."

Chaplain Cook says faith like this is what gives a soldier hope, an edge, a difference. "It's a privilege to be able to see a soldier accept Jesus, get to baptize him, disciple him in study and prayer, and see him grow to witness [to others] himself," says Cook. "He discovers it's God who is with him and will never forsake him. God gives us confidence in our salvation, so if we do die, we will be with our Lord. We need not fear.

"We're here, fighting for freedom and peace. We know, however, only true freedom and peace comes from God, 'because the Spirit's law of life in Christ Jesus has set us free from the law of sin and of death,'" he quotes from Romans 8:2.

"True freedom doesn't give us the liberty to do whatever we want," Cook said. In reality, "*destruction* is near when 'each man does what was right in his own eyes.' Freedom is not the absence of boundaries, but rather knowing how to operate within the parameters God has set.

"The Christian life is this freedom: a *greater* freedom to experience the abundant and eternal life God designed for us."

And they are experiencing this every day. Even in Iraq.

HAPPY FATHER'S DAY DADDY!

Katherine Anne's Hands 6/19/02   4 years old

HAPPY FATHER'S DAY DADDY!

Mary Lisette's Hands 6/19/02  7mos. old

# WHEN THOUGHTS TURN TOWARD HOME

## HUSBANDS AND WIVES, MOMS AND DADS

T he forty-eight-hour deadline President Bush gave Iraqi dictator Saddam Hussein came and went. The war was in motion. The thoughts of thousands of American families immediately turned to their loved ones overseas.

Concern for a brother in Kuwait.

Worry for a husband at the Iraqi border.

Fear for a wife serving on the front line.

Relief was all Laurie Hawks, in Chesapeake, Virginia, could feel. Operation Iraqi Freedom had finally started. She knew eventually it would end.

That's when her husband, Gene, a logistics officer assigned to the USS *Harry S. Truman*, would finally come home.

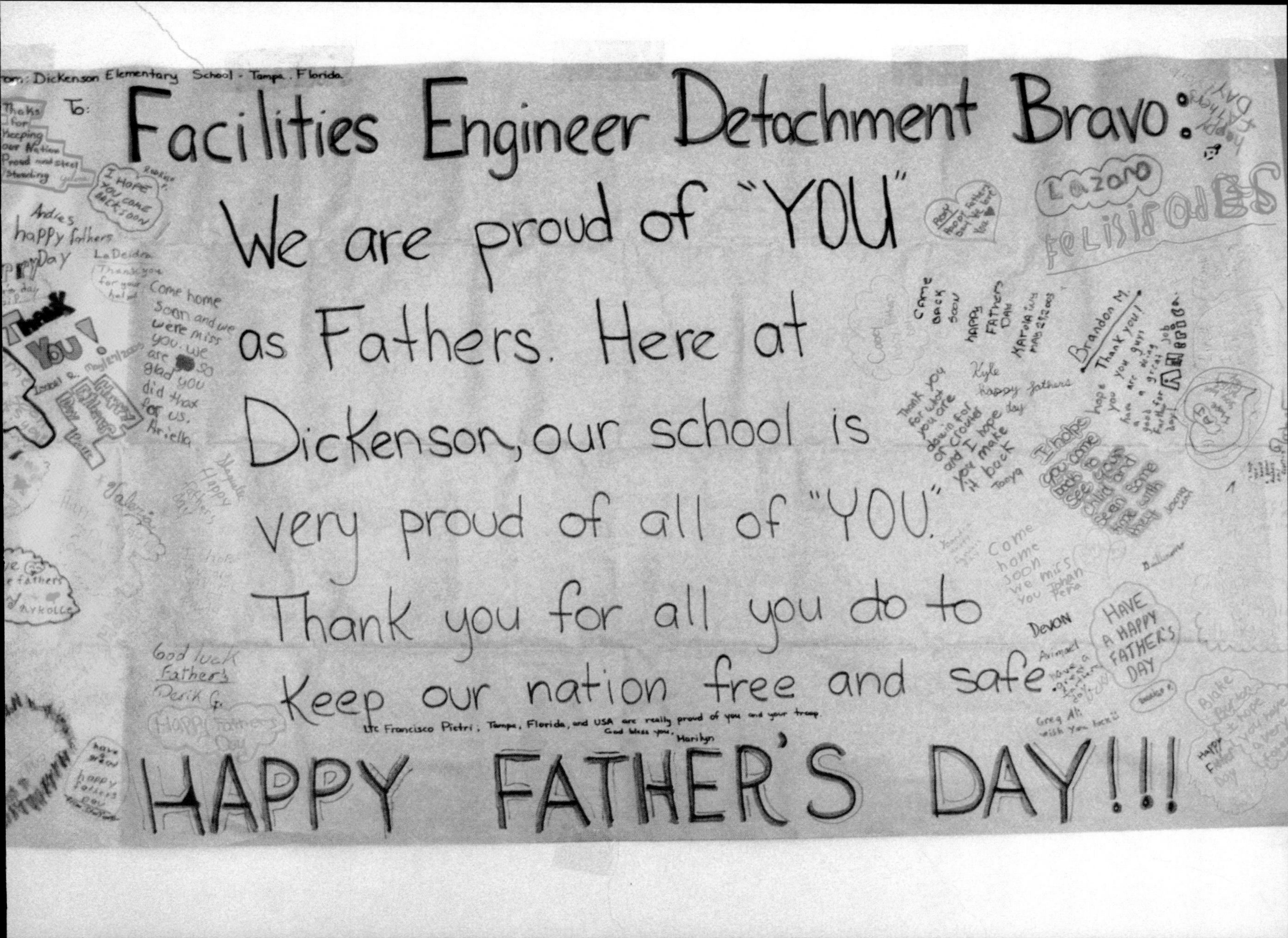
From: Dickenson Elementary School - Tampa, Florida.
To:
Facilities Engineer Detachment Bravo:
We are proud of "YOU" as Fathers. Here at Dickenson, our school is very proud of all of "YOU".
Thank you for all you do to Keep our nation free and safe.
LTC Francisco Pietri; Tampa, Florida, and USA are really proud of you and your troop. God bless you. Marilyn
HAPPY FATHER'S DAY!!!
I HOPE YOU COME BACK SOON
Come home soon and we were miss you. we are so glad you did thax for us. Ariella
Good luck Father's Derik G.
Come home soon we miss you Johan Pena
HAVE A HAPPY FATHER'S DAY
Thank you for what you are doing for our country and I hope you make it back Tonya
Devon
Brandon M. Thank you! you guys are doing a great job
Come back soon HAPPY FATHERS DAY

# WHEN DADDIES
# HAVE TO LEAVE

Good-byes for adults can be difficult. Good-byes for children can be devastating, both for the parent and the child.

Gene and Laurie Hawks celebrated Christmas 2002 with their little girls, Katherine and Mary . . . over Thanksgiving weekend. Gene was scheduled to ship out for an undetermined length of time and an undisclosed location. The night before his departure, the family gathered on board the *Truman.*

They tried to make the best of it. Gene's father, a thirty-year veteran, and his mother came along, and they'd toured the carrier. The family ate dinner together and decorated a small Christmas tree for Gene in his officer's stateroom. Now they were back in the minivan, saying their last good-byes as the chilly Norfolk evening grew later.

Five-year-old Katherine wasn't happy.

"But why does daddy have to leave?" she asked for the fifth time, tears streaming down her face. Gene patiently tried explaining where he was going though he knew his little girl didn't understand.

He tried hard to assure her he would be home soon. Then it was kisses and hugs, and Laurie drove the family car home, minus one very important passenger.

Gene admires her courage and sym-pathizes with the burdens she carries. "The toughest job in the Navy is that of a Navy spouse," he says, sitting in the officer's wardroom having lunch on board the *Truman,* somewhere in the East Mediterranean.

"I come out and do the same job I do back at the base, but Laurie's at home taking care of the house, the yard, the vehicle. It's a lot for one person to handle, but she doesn't complain."

Married for eleven of the fourteen years Gene has served in the Navy, this is their second deployment to experience but the first as parents. Both agree it's a lot harder this time around.

"Now that we're almost five months into the deployment, the rough days are more frequent," admits Laurie. "It is really tough trying to handle all the responsibility by myself and not only worry about *my* heartstrings but the heartstrings of my five-year-old as well."

Not long after Gene left, Laurie began making frequent trips to the emergency room with Mary, their one-year-old, for problems breathing. Doctors later concluded she was suffering from asthma, but there were early indications she might have something much more serious. Gene says God drove him to his knees when he heard they were testing Mary for illnesses like cystic fibrosis.

"That whole situation really forced me to rely on God," says Gene. "You get out *here,* and your job is to make things happen. But things like this make you realize you're not in control."

> **"That whole situation really forced me to rely on God. You get out *here,* and your job is to make things happen. Things like this make you realize you're not in control."**
>
> **Gene Hawks**

Their church back home goes a long way toward making this out-of-control feeling more bearable. Laurie and Gene, members of Pleasant Grove Baptist Church in Chesapeake, have experienced a huge outpouring of love and support from these Christian friends.

"They sent me a tape of their Christmas cantata awhile back, which Laurie sang in," says Gene. Different members of the church have also sent Gene cards or care packages, just to let him know he's missed. At home, Laurie receives help with yard work, babysitting, and plumbing problems.

"First and foremost, our church has been such a blessing through prayer," says Laurie, not to mention "the simple things, like asking how Gene is. I try to make it a point to specifically tell him who asks about him through the week. It lets him know he's not forgotten and that our church family does think about him and recognize he's not there."

And that he's coming home one day . . . to see two little girls whose daddy is doing the hard work of freedom.

It's ok Misty. Daddy's almost home!

# JUST PASSING THROUGH

You wouldn't think of Nancy McClure as the grand-mother-type if you saw her. It's not often you see a grandmother sporting desert camouflage.

A National Guard reservist with the 168th Military Police Battalion stationed at the Falcon Forward Base, south of Baghdad, McClure's youthful face and frequent smile hide her forty-two years well. But it doesn't bother her a bit to tell a visitor that both of her grown daughters are expecting babies. She just hopes she can make it home to Lebanon, Missouri, before her grandchildren are born.

McClure signed up for the Reserves when she was thirty-nine and turned forty during basic training. "They tell me I might be the oldest nonmilitary basic trainee," she says proudly. She tried joining when she was thirty-seven but was told she was too old. When her daughters looked into enlisting two years later, their recruiter confirmed for her she also could enlist.

"It was rough in basics," she admits, reaching for the Rose of Sharon hanging from a chain around her neck, a necklace she bought during her initial training. "When you're forty, you don't pray for each day. You pray for each step!"

> **"This world is not my home, I'm just passing through. I tell the other soldiers that there is no place on earth that's really home; we've got a heavenly home to look forward to."**
>
> **Nancy McClure**

She remembers the last road march her training group took. She'd twisted her knee the day before and was struggling. So she started praying and didn't stop—all the way to the end. She credits God with getting her through, then and now. In Iraq.

It's a place she's serving by her own choosing.

"They were asking for volunteers from my unit, so I raised my hand," McClure remembers. "They didn't take me seriously at first. Everyone was telling me to put my hand down. But I wanted to go. The Lord really touched my heart for the young soldiers I trained with. They'd say, 'If you can make it, I know I can.'"

A member of Tabernacle Baptist Church at home, McClure celebrated her twenty-fifth wedding anniversary in November while in Baghdad. She acknowledges the military and the ministry are in her blood, both of which can be attributed to her husband, a former Baptist pastor who served in the Army early on in their marriage.

"He's my anchor, my partner, and my biggest fan and supporter," McClure says, her eyes lighting up. "He says, 'I miss you terribly, but I'm so proud of you.'"

While there are light moments sprinkled in, such as finding humor in the type of missions she conducts for her unit ("I do the laundry," she laughs), she acknowledges that in a war setting one's frailties become obvious. She says God has shown her that she can't do it all by herself, that she needs other people. And other people need her.

When life seems hardest in this desert environment, far from her loved ones back in Missouri, one song in particular keeps her going.

"This world is not my home, I'm just passing through," she quotes. "I tell the other soldiers that there is no place on earth that's really home. We've got a heavenly home to look forward to."

Finished with her reflections, McClure stands up, anxious to keep her next appointment. She's been training and learning the sport of boxing the last two months. Her first match is tomorrow.

Something to teach the grandkids.

# When You Can't Go Home

Chaplain (Captain) Timothy Stansberry is a battalion chaplain with the 422nd Civil Affairs Army Reserve unit based out of Greensboro, North Carolina. He's also a bivocational pastor for Trinity Baptist Church in Long Island, New York, and a hospital chaplain before being activated for service in Iraq.

While their entrance into Iraq was quiet, it was still chaotic. Not a single light was on in the neighborhood; there were no checkpoints, and destroyed cars lined the streets. As a civil affairs unit, they went to work immediately trying to get water and electricity back, putting together some semblance of order.

Stansberry, who received a bronze star for his service during the combat phase of Operation Iraqi Freedom, performed chaplain duties as he could. He set up on the tailgate of a Humvee, offering communion, passing out New Testaments, and reading a passage of Scripture with his soldiers.

He says the biggest surprise for him has been dealing with family issues for the troops. "I thought when we got into combat that would take primary focus, but it hasn't been the case," he explains. While all soldiers struggle with issues at home during a deployment, reservists particularly can have a hard time with being away.

"People carry their worries from home—they worry about bills, about family members," he adds. "You get that one e-mail, that one letter, and it makes it really difficult to think of nothing else but home. There's very little they can do [about those problems] here; my job is to listen, offer counsel as I can."

**"People carry their worries from home—they worry about bills, about family members. You get that one e-mail, that one letter, and it makes it really difficult to think of nothing else but home."**

Captain Timothy Stansberry

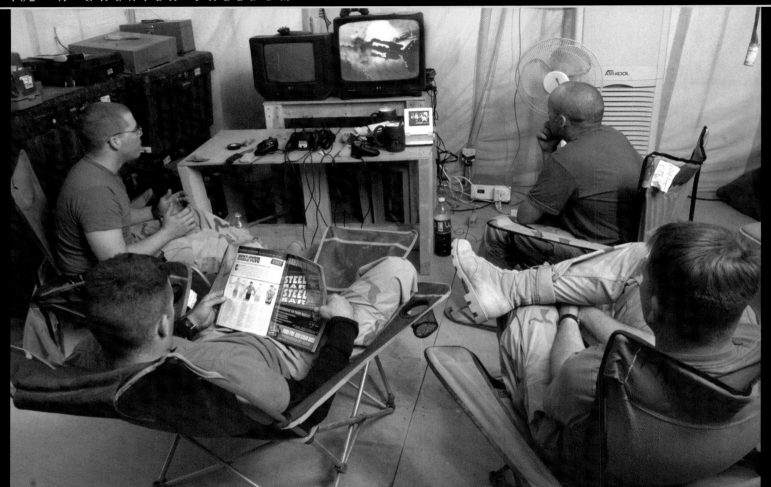

## Gifts from Far Away

Sergeant 1st Class Michael Yarber, 372nd Mobile Public Affairs Detachment from an Army Reserves unit in Nashville, Tennessee, looks through a recent care package sent from home. Packages and letters from friends and family mean everything to a deployed soldier.

# A DREAM HOMECOMING

It was the early morning hours of April 5, 2003—Eastern Standard Time—and Jennifer Cook's cell phone was ringing.

"Jen, it's Eddie. Where are you?"

"Well, Eddie, it's three a.m. I'm at the hospital."

Jennifer was about to give birth to the couple's first child. Her husband, Chaplain (Captain) Eddie Cook, was thousands of miles away, serving with his men in Iraq. He'd left when she was seven months pregnant, on Valentine's Day.

"The whole thing with the military is inevitably they're going to miss a birth, a birthday, something," says Jennifer. "You have to know how to deal with it."

The couple had discussed the important details before he'd deployed. They'd agreed on a name, they'd found a doula, ensuring she'd have ample care and support, but there was still a wide range of mixed emotions. "Like with anything, though, we knew the Lord would make a way and watch over us all," she says.

That early April night, Eddie called back two more times. Finally, after a twenty-seven-hour labor, Edward Jonathan Cook was born.

Daddy's boy.

Only daddy wasn't there. Jennifer admits the first six weeks after Edward was born were the hardest. Though her mother stayed for two weeks, and some other family members came and helped out, it was still hard not to feel alone.

"Those six weeks, just being a new mom, the nonstop sleepless nights were extremely hard," she says. "As much as I wanted to cry and scream right along with my newborn, I gave it to the Lord, and He got me through."

Jennifer grew up in Jasper, Indiana, and met Eddie while they were both serving on the mission field in North Africa. They married in 1999, and Eddie rejoined the 82nd Airborne Division in 2002 as a chaplain. Now thirty-one and watching her little boy grow up, she's experiencing that exciting mix of joy and laughter. Yet it's bittersweet because her husband isn't here to share it.

At times, it's downright heart wrenching.

Edward started giggling when he was four months old. One night when Eddie was on the phone, his wife told him, "You've got to hear this!"

"I got Edward giggling, and he was just cackling, but when I picked up the phone again, Eddie was quiet and said 'Jen, stop, you're making me cry.' Every guy is different, but you have to be careful how much you share."

It wasn't until after her husband deployed that Jennifer truly learned what it meant to turn something completely over to God. She originally struggled with her role as a chaplain's wife. Should she start a Bible study? Lead a support group? Do something spiritually big and visible?

The answer she got from the Lord was to wait. After the men deployed, she felt God calling her to start a weekly ladies prayer service. She's seeing the help it gives to others as well as herself.

"Occasionally, I hear explosions in the background when I'm talking to him on the phone," she says (adding that Eddie thinks, *It's the niftiest thing that I can hear all that*). You go to bed thinking someone is going to knock on my door or call me in the middle of the night to tell me something's happened. Eventually you realize you have to put it in the hands of God."

Jennifer says God has given her a peace that no harm will come to her husband. She's seen other women with strong faith feel the same thing.

"There're women who call me saying they cry every day for their husbands, and they don't know the Lord," she says. "You've got me and others who can't explain the peace we're feeling" by any measurement of human willpower.

There *have* been really tough moments. When Eddie called home to tell her he was on the list to get two weeks of R&R because he was a new father, they were overjoyed—only to find out a few days later he'd been taken off the list because he was an officer. No officers would be granted leave.

"I had to take a few days to vent to the Lord, but eventually—once again—I had to praise Him," Jennifer says, admitting it wasn't easy. "I'm thankful we have a healthy baby boy, Eddie is safe, and that we're on the downside of this deployment."

She now sees that God has called both Eddie and her into ministry and that sacrifices are sometimes a necessary part of it. The war in Iraq is about much more than giving others their physical freedom or stopping a dictator. It's about God sculpting His people, chiseling them down to their basic needs, leaving them with nothing to stand in the way of their Christlikeness beaming through.

"God showed me Luke 9:62 a few weeks ago" [where Jesus says, 'No one who puts his hand to the plow and looks back is fit for the kingdom of God'], "and I realized that we are not working for the Army but for the kingdom," she says.

"That requires a forward walk, not turning around and looking at frustrations or missed opportunities. Our vision is eternal not temporal. I am learning more and more by this deployment that I have a daily choice to be positive or negative. Truth is, I can be both, but I am learning."

Back in Baghdad, Chaplain Cook acknowledges the difficulty in not seeing his little boy. But he knows God is providing a spiritual bond between them. He has lots of plans for when he does return.

There can be no doubt that Edward knows his daddy's voice. Since his son was born, Eddie calls home every chance he gets, to sing "Jesus Loves Me" to his little boy. His young son's face lights up with an enormous grin every time he hears him.

"I want to teach Edward about our Lord Jesus Christ and to be a God-fearing young man," says Cook. "I want to teach him the truth of the Bible, teach him how to camp, how to shoot, and how to enjoy the outdoors."

He can't wait for the day when he sees his son face to face.

He knows just how it will be.

"The first thing I'll do is let him hear my voice, let him hear me sing 'Jesus Loves Me' to him, as I've done so many times on the phone," Cook says. His eyes tear up, imagining the meeting he's been thinking about since he first heard the cries of his son from so far away on the other side of the world. "Then I'll reach out to him, and I'll take him into my arms, and I'll hold him.

"And maybe I'll even sing it to him again."

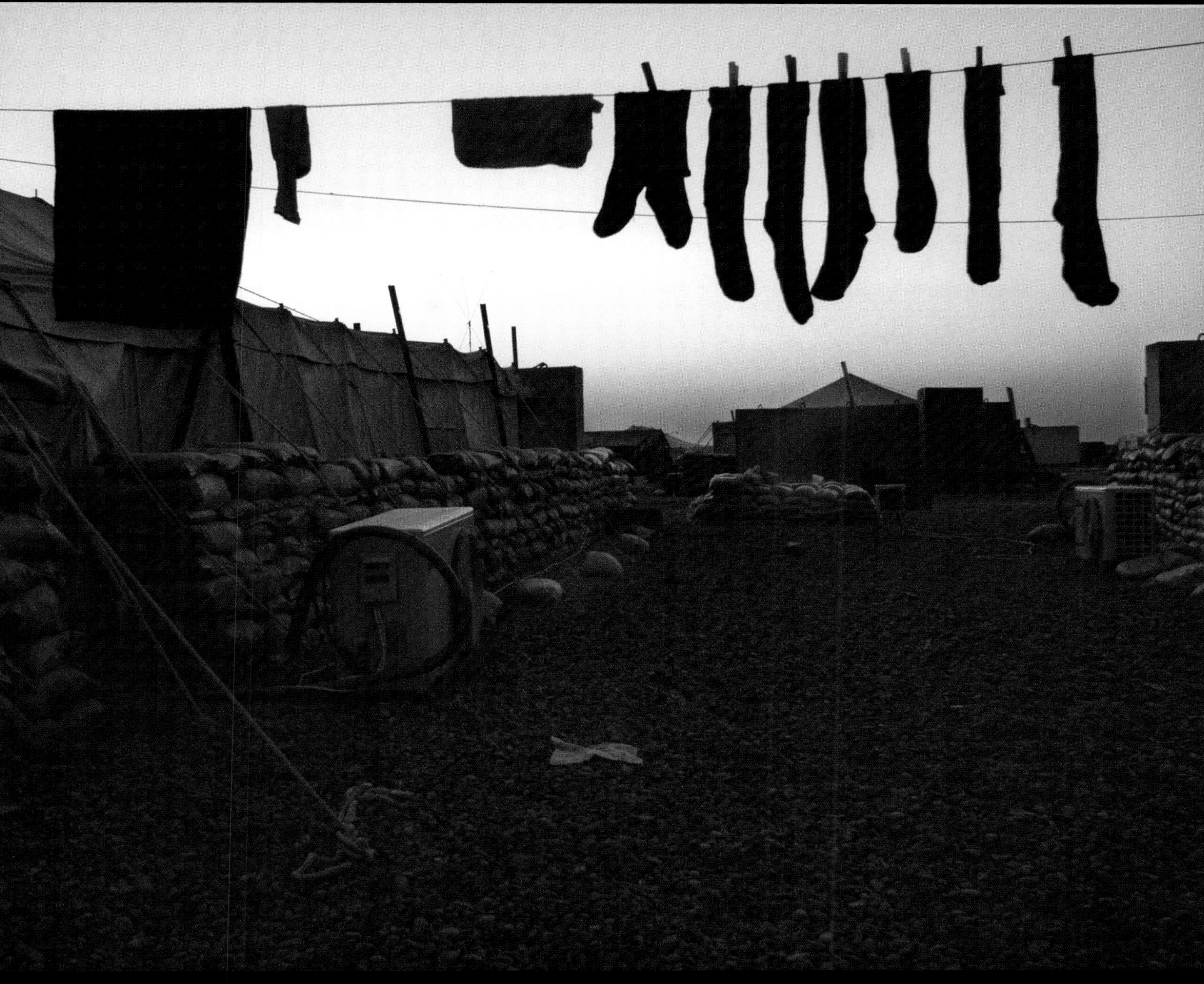

Photograph courtesy of Maj. Carroll Harris, USMC

# I KNOW WHERE I'M GOING

## A MEMORIAL TRIBUTE

A pair of light armored vehicles driven by the deceased soldier's fellow crewmen are angled at forty-five degrees, left and right, the hood of each vehicle pointing to a makeshift cross hand-hewn from available timber.

A cross. Always a cross.

The soldier's personal items are displayed. His binoculars, a CD player, something that reminds his friends of who he was, what he did, how he lived.

The platoon assembles in formation. The commanding officer orders them to attention. The fallen soldier's name is read in a roll call, having "died with honor on the field of battle."

The reality of it all begins to set in with a vengeance. He was here. Suddenly, without warning, he's gone. It's surreal, nearly unbelievable. The exacting price of freedom.

One by one, Marines break from formation, each carrying one of his buddy's effects. First his M-16, fixed bayonet plunged into the sand, its stock pointing toward the sky. Next, the very pair of boots he was wearing at the time of his death. Next, his Kevlar helmet, carefully placed atop the rifle, suspended motionless in the air. Then another member of his platoon hangs his fellow crewman's dog tags on the grip of the rifle.

There is silence. Long, terrible silence.

Then the same four soldiers come to a poncho-covered podium, each to deliver—whether in prepared remarks or heartfelt spontaneity—their final words of gratitude and honor for this member of their unit. It's like a right arm being tugged from their own bodies, a loss too deep for words, yet crying out for something to be said. These brief accounts about their fallen friend bring low chuckles or warm tears to red eyes, leaving wet streaks trailing down their silent, dusty faces. These are not stories from the distant past but minutes-old memories that will hopefully find their way back to family and friends, to children and grandchildren who will ask about this war, who will want to know more, who will wonder why and how and where and when.

They pray. They are called again to attention. They say farewell to their fallen comrade with a crisp salute.

They return to rest.

They return to duty.

## A Salute to Courage

This type of service—or some form or variation of it, whatever is expedient to the situation in which soldiers find themselves—has been conducted countless times through-

Photograph courtesy of SGT Eric R. Poole, USMC

out the annals of America's history, and those fighting for freedom in the dust and grime of the Iraqi desert have sadly seen their share of these.

This simple display—the boots, the helmet, the unmanned rifle—possesses overwhelming meaning each time it is assembled before somber faces gathered in the surrounding circle. A life has been taken. A fallen soldier has paid the greatest sacrifice any soldier, airman, sailor, or Marine can make . . . for the sake of the mission. For the sanctity of freedom. For an ideal greater than oneself.

With little in the way of similarities, these memorials are a far cry from the funerals we're accustomed to attending over the years in the come-and-go of our lives. These makeshift services are conducted wherever one happens to be, on ground not necessarily set apart for burial rites. Those gathered around have had no time to shave and shower for the occasion, much less don their finest. These proceedings are made difficult by their all-too-necessary abruptness, by their out-of-character surroundings, by the threat of danger that hovers around all of those who watch and weep and wish this didn't have to be.

These are among the "most painful experiences I've ever been a part of," says Sergeant Eric Poole, 3rd LAR Battalion, 1st Marine Division. The only relief comes in knowing that God is at work here, that "we truly are liberating the Iraqis from a terrible future."

Navy Chaplain Commander Frank Holley, who has presided at a number of these services during his time in Iraq, reveals another aspect of the mood that pervades them. "Any time you have a memorial service, there's a sense of bonding, a sense of family that even transcends [what one feels] as a Christian. It's something unique to the military." Much like the shared camaraderie that exists at the funeral of a police officer or firefighter, "men or women who routinely lay their lives on the line have a special bonding in a particular situation. They are like a band of

Photograph courtesy of SGT Eric R. Poole, USMC

brothers. Not until you go off to combat together can you get the sense of it."

Holley, who served at the war's forward line as the regimental chaplain for the 5th Marine Regiment, one of the divisions responsible for the fall of Baghdad, understands the many emotions and reactions that settle in after the death of a fallen friend. Endorsed by the United Methodist church, he's been in the chaplain corps for almost twenty years.

He understands, too, that even though a relative few will suffer death at the hands of war and its enemies, such nearness to death is a reality they all must face.

## Living with Death

Holley vividly remembers the night before his unit crossed the line of departure into Iraq. He did his best to move quickly to each group of men, praying with them as the sun lowered and the air strikes began.

"I remember wondering how many guys would remember about this night, years down the road, and look back and think of the chaplains and other Christians who prayed for them," he says.

As he watched oil fires burning, he thought of the letters he had written to his wife and his three children—letters he hoped they would never have to read alone—letters that told them how much he loved them, how proud he was of them, what an honor it was to be their father, her husband. He had left these letters in safekeeping back in Kuwait, "just in case something happened."

You never know.

But Holley knew one thing. Like the fallen heroes who had put their trust in Christ while bravely performing their duties and carrying out their missions, fear was not a motivating concern for him. God's peace was enough, available in ample measures, as He had promised in the Scriptures.

"I never feared for my life, the entire time over there," Holley says, although he admits "when something blows up near you, it gets your attention. But when I die, I know where I'm going. I know I have the peace that passes understanding."

It's a peace he tries to pass on to the people he serves.

There were many nights on the road to Baghdad that a group would gather by the hood of his Humvee for prayer. Some nights there were fifteen, other times as many as forty men, arms around each other, praying to God for strength and protection.

"Soldiers facing the possibility of death yearn for a sense of purpose, for something absolute in their lives," Holley says. "Christians have that assurance. You can still be an effective soldier without being a spiritual person, but I don't think you're completed."

Those who possess a belief in Jesus Christ do indeed know where they're going. They have a peace that replaces fear. It doesn't have anything to do with a map, a compass, or the superiority of their weapons and technology. Christians in the military know the One who has saved them—the One who will take them to their final destination when their appointed time comes—even if it comes on this unfamiliar side of the world, surrounded only by their buddies in battle.

> **"Soldiers facing the possibility of death yearn for a sense of purpose, for something absolute in their lives. Christians have that assurance."**
>
> **Commander Frank Holley**

Death is the last thing they want, but they know it is not the last word for them.

Truly, a greater freedom beats within the human heart when Christ's forgiveness has already been longed for and received. There's a peace that pervades the innermost emotions, deeper than any fear or worry that comes with being in the midst of war.

God has given His peace to these soldiers who have served and given their lives for others—those who have received by faith His gift of salvation and who now experience His peace firsthand in the glorious realm of heaven. Eternal life is His reward—not for their courage and bravery, not for their honor and duty—but for their simple acceptance of who they were without Him, of what He did on the cross to wash away their sins, and of what He did in the empty tomb to make their death a pathway to life.

He brings peace to the families who weep for the loss of their loved one. He understands their pain. He felt the same when He watched His Son die, stretched out on a cross, the Son who later rose from the dead so that none of us have to experience the depths of hell if we believe in Him.

"'O Death, where is your victory?

O Death, where is your sting?'

"Now the sting of death is sin, and the power of sin is the law. But thanks be to God, who gives us the victory through our Lord Jesus Christ!" (1 Cor. 15:55–57).

All who have lived in Him can rest in His peace.

# THE ROAD TO DEMOCRACY

## LIFE AFTER SADDAM

Some call him a modern-day Nebuchadnezzar. For more than twenty-four years, Saddam Hussein ruled Iraq with a dictator's recipe made up of equal parts fear and murder, crippling Iraq's twenty-four million citizens under a deep-rooted organized approach of paranoia and fear. His presence was everywhere—on buildings, posters, in schoolbooks, and other publications. If it wasn't his photo, it was his name, his signature, his initials, woven into the architecture of gates, adorning walls and doors. You couldn't escape his face.

You also couldn't escape his ears. His intelligence officers and spies came in many forms. Your next door neighbor. Your friend from church. Always, looking for any signs of disloyalty to Saddam. A culture of bribes and lying pervaded the country.

His opulent palaces filled with gold, crystal, and the finest things money could purchase dotted the countryside. His expensive taste came at the detriment of the Iraqi people, who depended on family members outside of Iraq to send money home so they could buy food for another month.

School children were conditioned to greet the dictator during his rare appearances by jumping up and saying, "We love you, Saddam." State-controlled television and radio stations provided daily brainwashing for the adults. Personal satellites for homes were illegal, punishable by heavy fines and up to four years in prison.

Though powerful in appearance, Saddam was insecure in his safety. So worried was he about possible assassination attempts, each palace chef was required to fix three elaborate meals every day in order to keep would-be assas-sins guessing on the Iraqi ruler's comings and goings—food going uneaten while Iraqis starved in the streets.

Then U.S. and coalition forces invaded. The tyrant predicted the war would bring great bloodshed for the Americans and end victoriously for Iraq, but only four short weeks later, he and the rest of his army were on the run. Baghdad was no longer his. He was a fugitive in his own country.

Eight months later, on December 13, U.S. forces found him, grubby and disheveled, at the bottom of a narrow dark

hole between two rooms of a mud shack, nine miles from his hometown of Tikrit. He told the soldiers, "I am Saddam Hussein. I am the president of Iraq. I want to negotiate."

Standing there, squinting in the sunlight, his appearance had changed considerably since the day before the first bombs dropped on Baghdad in the spring. His graying beard was long and bushy and his hair matted. Even with his altered appearance, his defiance remained the same.

With his capture, Iraqis breathed easier. Despite the progress they've seen by the assistance of U.S. and coalition forces, there has always been that underlying fear evoked by the ruler himself. The unanswered questions that subconsciously halted full cooperation and kept Iraqis from helping even themselves were: *What if he comes back? What if his people come back to power?*

But seeing their former ruler emerge from a spider hole, caught like a rat in a trap, Iraqis are looking forward to the future, to new beginnings, to a possible democracy.

There's still a long way to go. Insurgents aren't making it easy. It is a difficult process.

But there is hope. For a better life. For better opportunities. For a greater freedom.

**Beds line the interior of what once was Saddam Hussein's "missile room," which served as the ending point of the lives of many. Said to have been the place where people were either promoted or shot on sight, it's now used to protect. People who were displaced after the Al Rashid Hotel bombing now live there.**

As work to rebuild Iraq continues, Saddam's former governmental palace now serves as headquarters for the Coalition Provisional Authority. Shortly after this photo was taken, four statues of the former dictator's head sitting atop CPA head-quarters were removed from the compound.

## Life Goes On

With the combat phase of the war over, life goes on for the people of Baghdad. Neighbors continue to look out for each other, and street vendors have returned to business as usual. Life is an ever-revolving process, destined to keep moving forward despite adversity that visits along the way.

# A GREATER FREEDOM

## NEW LIFE IN IRAQ

As soon as he opened the door, Dhakir* knew he wasn't going to have a choice about leaving with the men who came to get him. And he knew he wouldn't be coming back "in an hour," as they were telling him.

Saddam's security agents stood just outside Dhakir's small home where he, his wife, Raja, and their two teenagers lived in the center of Baghdad. "Don't open your mouth and don't make any sudden movement," they commanded him. "Just walk to the car and get in," pointing to an unmarked government vehicle idling on the street. The back passenger door was open, making the ominous point to Dhakir that this was a ride he had little say in.

Night was falling, and lights from the surrounding houses on Dhakir's street glowed through the dusky twilight of the evening. His eyes darted, quickly taking in the scene, his attention now falling on another man who was standing there—a man from his church—who pointed his finger at Dhakir.

"Yes, that is Dhakir—he's the one who gave me the audiocassettes," he said, before abruptly leaving.

*Some names have been changed

Standing at the doorway in his pajamas and robe, Dhakir knew he had to think fast.

"I can't go out like this," he said, tugging at his bed-clothes. "Let me run upstairs and change," he protested.

The men shook their heads, pointing to Dhakir's son, Basim ("smiling" in English), who had unsuspectingly come to the door to see who his father was talking to.

Let the boy go get his father some clothes, the men ordered.

Soon Dhakir's hands and feet were hard at work dressing himself in front of his surprise guests, his mind also at work—whirling, spinning, covering his bases. He knew he had to talk to his wife before he left the house. She had to know what to do with that mountain of Christian CDs and cassettes sitting in a pile on the floor of their living room, covered only by a curtain. Everyone knew it was illegal to run a preaching center out of a private residence under Saddam's regime, and he had to think of a way—fast—to protect his family from further harm.

Desperately needing an excuse for delay, the quick-thinking Iraqi complained to the men that the sweater he was wearing had a hole in it. To his surprise—and breath-less relief—they relented. Dhakir bolted upstairs . . . to see his wife.

And to save his gospel media ministry.

## Bringing the Gospel to Iraq

Dhakir was born into a Mandaean family, part of a culture and religion that goes back thousands of years to the days of John the Baptist, who, at the time of his death, had four hundred disciples still following him.

"John the Baptist told his followers to follow Jesus," Dhakir explains. "Ninety percent did, but ten percent refused." Those refusing to become disciples of Jesus formed their own religion, worshiping John the Baptist instead of Jesus Christ. To this day, the ceremony of baptism makes up a large part of Mandaean religious rituals.

But in 1994, at the age of thirty-six, Dhakir says Jesus appeared to him in a dream, and as a result of this revelation, Dhakir accepted Christ as his Savior. Not long after this, his brother, who had previously left Iraq for Australia, sent him a Bible. And by the end of the next year, Dhakir—an electrical engineer for the government by day—felt God calling him to preach the gospel. By whatever means necessary.

The problem was, since only licensed churches were allowed to exist, preaching Christianity without permission of the Iraqi dictatorship could mean a minimum of three years in prison. And Saddam's agents, who constantly looked for anything that might oppose the dictator's rule, frequently attended these churches to check things like this out. Dhakir's family attended the only Arabic protestant church in Baghdad, dating back to 1953. The church, according to Dhakir, was filled with people who worked for and were extremely loyal to Saddam. Even the church council was made up almost entirely of members of the Baath party, the Arab socialist group where Saddam got his political start.

> **"I didn't know a lot about the Holy Spirit at the time, but now looking back, I realize it was truly the Holy Spirit leading me when I decided to start a media ministry."**
>
> **Dhakir**

"I didn't know a lot about the Holy Spirit at the time, but now looking back, I realize it was truly the Holy Spirit leading me when I decided to start a media ministry," says Dhakir.

He surmised: "everyone has a cassette player of some kind in their home." It was truly one of the easiest, most effective ways to preach the gospel in Iraq because the entire family could receive the message of Christ without putting themselves at risk.

They started with forty blank tapes. Dhakir regularly stayed up into the wee hours of the morning, waiting to tape Christian broadcasts he could pick up on his radio. His wife then made copies of the programs on their small double-deck cassette player that sat on the kitchen counter while she made dinner each evening. They'd take the tapes to church on Fridays, carrying them in white canvas bags and passing them out after the service.

Eventually, though, the tapes ran out, and Dhakir turned to the Bible for wisdom in knowing what to do next. He read Malachi 3:7-12, which talked about giving 10 percent of one's income to God.

"You have to be honest to the Lord," says Dhakir. So he and his family began setting aside 10 percent of their income to purchase new resources for the ministry. He soon started frequenting the Baghdad marketplace, looking for secondhand tapes that could be recycled—buying so many, in fact, that he was able to negotiate a better price. He even started using 10 percent of the money he received from his mother and brothers, who—like almost all Iraqi nationals living outside the country—were sending financial support to their families at home. "This was a very hard time for Iraqis, before the war," Dhakir explains. "Salaries weren't high enough for people to live on."

Yet Dhakir was obedient to God. And seeing results.

## A Meeting with the Council

It wasn't long before Dhakir's growing ministry got noticed. His church council began to grow concerned at the number of tapes Dhakir was handing out and the number of people responding to the ministry. They called him in for a meeting.

It seemed more like a court trial.

"Your active ministry is causing a problem for us," they told him. "We are afraid Saddam will close the church."

The council's nine members told Dhakir that new rules were being created that would force his ministry to be reorganized, and until those policies were in place, the ministry must stop.

Dhakir, however, had no intention of stopping.

"I did my ministry in the shadow," he admits. Even his wife helped, by bringing tapes and video copies to her women's Bible study meetings.

A month later, he was called back to meet with the council a second time. They discovered that Dhakir was listed as a Mandaean instead of a Christian in government records. Dhakir explained that though he had been born Mandaean, he had indeed accepted Christ along with his family. The council insisted he get his religious status changed on his record if he wanted to continue his ministry. So for two months he went to the Iraqi courts again and again, trying unsuccessfully to get this one word changed on his official identification documents.

"Iraqi courts are full of bribes . . . if you want to get anything done quickly," Dhakir says. "I follow Jesus. I don't pay bribes."

Finally, at the end of the second month, he was able to get a meeting with the court judges.

"Why do you want to switch to Christianity? Why not switch to Islam?" the Muslim judges badgered Dhakir. Yet he persisted in his intentions, refusing to deny his faith or further complicate his ministry.

At last, his request was granted. It seemed as though his ministry could now succeed. With his papers now in order, the council even gave Dhakir a small room in the church where he could house his tapes. And each Friday—Iraq's holy day of the week—people would flock there to borrow sermons and Bible studies from him.

## Each Friday—Iraq's holy day of the week—people would flock there to borrow sermons and Bible studies from him.

The room, which used to be a tiny kitchen, now resembled a media center. Copies of CDs covered an old freezer. Audiocassettes lined the top of a small, rickety table. As word spread, his mailing list and the number of people borrowing tapes and videos grew to as many as ten thousand.

"It truly was a source of blessings," Dhakir says, smiling as he remembers.

Those blessings, however, would once again come under fire.

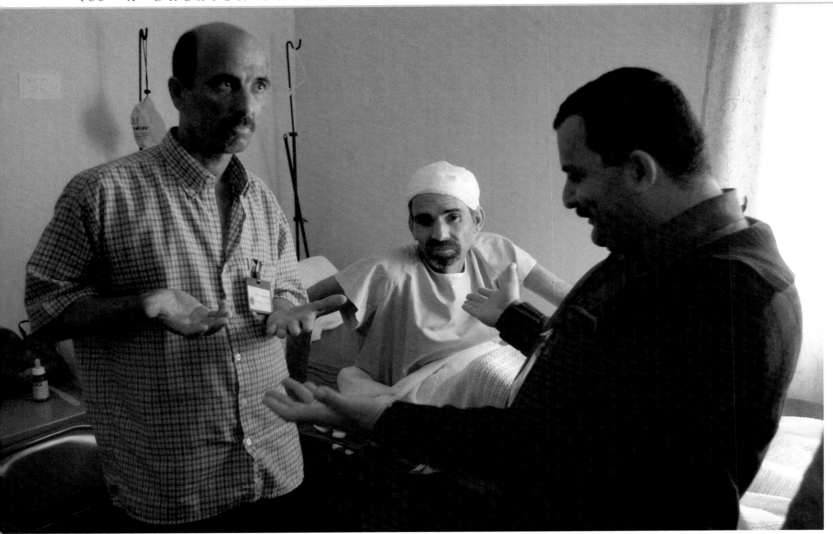

**"Americans are angels,"** this Iraqi man (left) says as Dhakir interprets. He and his brother were injured in a welding accident while working for the military. Taken to a military hospital in Baghdad, the man has recovered, and his brother is close to being released. If he had been in an Iraqi hospital, the man says, his arms would have been cut off. He expresses gratitude for the American doctors and nurses who took care of them.

Right: Dhakir shows the stack of flyers he has printed over the last eight years that includes the salvation message and testimonies of Iraqi Christians. More than 130,000 have been printed and distributed.

## Locked Doors

In September 2002, as the political waters between Iraq and the United States began to boil, Dhakir's ministry was flourishing. "The people didn't stop. They were taking tapes, and many lives were being changed," he says.

But the head of the church's council and his assistant, part of Saddam's intelligence force, began creating problems for Dhakir. They complained of a sermon that Dhakir was distributing by an Egyptian pastor who compared the Bible to the Koran.

"Your ministry must stop," they said.

But he would not stop. Dhakir and his wife continued to distribute the tapes and eventually began printing Iraqi flyers with the salvation message, copying six hundred the first week, then regularly a thousand a month on his computer printer at home.

In January 2003, he was called once again before the council.

"We have seen your flyer in Iraqi hospitals," they told Dhakir. "You are going to get our church closed. The Americans are about to come in. The ministry must not continue."

Dhakir left the meeting and went back to his house, praying in earnest for what God would have him do.

"The Lord told me, 'Go, don't stop.'"

> **"The Lord told me, 'Go, don't stop.'"** Dhakir

So the next Friday, January 31, 2003, he showed up at his little room in the church as usual. But this time the door was locked, and the head of the church council stood waiting for him.

"We don't want your ministry, and we don't want the gospel preached," the man said, unlocking the door of Dhakir's small media room, insisting he take his belongings elsewhere.

"But I haven't done anything wrong," Dhakir protested.

"You don't like to obey my orders, do you?" the man asked Dhakir.

"I don't like disobeying my Jesus," Dhakir replied, as he moved into the room to gather the offending tapes and take them home.

"I don't like disobeying my Jesus." Dhakir

Dhakir's children Lana (left), nineteen, and Basim, seventeen, read in the room they share adjacent to their parents bedroom seen through the open doorway. The family has lived in this house for more than twenty years.

Shards of glass line the top of a wall behind Dhakir's house, keeping would-be thieves at bay. Shortly after their tape ministry began, someone broke into their home while the family slept upstairs and stole all of Dhakir's equipment, causing the need for the glass along with heavier doors and deadbolts.

## Prison

Saddam's security agents arrived at his door the very next evening.

As his captors waited impatiently just inside the front door, Dhakir came running—in his holey sweater—into the upstairs room where Raja was ironing. She had heard the knock on the door but dismissed it as one of her son's friends.

Her eyes now widening at the horror of what was happening, she listened to her husband explain that he was being taken away by Saddam's men. She nodded her head as he instructed her to hide the tapes sitting on the floor of their living room.

In a terrifying instant, he was gone.

At first, there was no time to dwell on the sudden void filling her house or to think about what was happening to her husband. Raja quickly called for help from her neighbors, who descended on the house in a great rush to hide the tapes. Muslims, Mandaeans, and Christian neighbors alike all came to the family's aid. "In Iraqi culture, when it comes to protection of a neighbor, religion is thrown out," explains Raja. "They risked their lives for us."

After the mad dash to move the tapes had ended, Raja sat, exhausted, and prayed with her children. "I believed

**Raja never gave up in her belief that God would bring her husband home.**

what the men had said, that Dhakir would be back in an hour," Raja says.

But the hour turned into three.

Then three hours turned into the next day.

Raja (which means "hope") had at one time worked, like her husband, as an engineer for the government but quit to stay home with her children. In the late 1990s, she watched as their closest family members left the country, unable to endure the conditions in their country under Saddam's regime.

"The hardest moment was when I said good-bye to my sisters when they left for Holland," she says. "I could easily have become depressed, but Jesus filled us with a bigger purpose. Just living day by day, He filled us with a greater ambition to tell the people about His grace and His good news."

It was that bigger purpose that kept Raja going the day after Dhakir had been taken. "Jesus gave me a peace that Dhakir would come home."

Dhakir, however, had good reason to doubt. He found himself a prisoner in Saddam's intelligence prison, a facility known throughout Iraq for its horrible torture and senseless killings—not of criminals but of prisoners who were arrested for purely political reasons.

Dressed in prison garb and prison slippers, Dhakir shared a four-by-four-meter cell with five Muslims—three Shiite and two Sunni. He soon learned that ten evangelical pastors were arrested in all.

The time came for his first interrogation.

Blindfolded and hands tied, Dhakir was led to another room, where angry voices questioned him: "Why did you change your religion from Mandaean to Christianity? Why didn't you change it to Muslim? Don't you know that the Muslim religion is the best? Don't you know the prophet Muhammad is the last prophet who holds a complete message from God?"

Dhakir tried his best to answer. He kept his responses brief by explaining only that he had studied religions for the past several years. He had reached the conclusion that Christianity was the best fit based on his former religion, which worshiped John the Baptist, a follower of Christ.

His interrogators began talking to him about his media ministry, which was reportedly reaching various parts of Iraq, some very far away. Secret prayer meetings had been discovered where media supplied through Dhakir's ministry were being used, and as a result, several Muslims converted to Christianity.

> Secret prayer meetings had been discovered where media supplied through Dhakir's ministry were being used, and as a result, several Muslims had converted to Christianity.

"You are destroying the infrastructure of the Iraqi society by letting this happen!" his captors shouted. Silently, Dhakir began guessing the number of years he would be in prison. One of the prisoners in his cell had told him the minimum was fifteen.

Another officer then addressed him. Though Dhakir's eyes were covered, he could tell by the man's voice that he had a nervous temper and was extremely upset.

"One of the CDs you distributed belonged to an American preacher that talked about leaders and integrity," the officer stated. "Do you remember this?"

"I have hundreds of CDs in my ministry, but I think I remember parts of it," Dhakir answered honestly. "What's wrong with it?"

"This preacher claims that the best leaders in the world should be faithful Christians. This means that Saddam Hussein, the Muslim, will have no chance to be leader of the world!" the man hissed in Dhakir's ear.

Dhakir could hear his heart pounding. At that moment he realized what they were intending to accuse him with—treason against Saddam. The only punishment for such a serious charge: death by execution.

Adequately ridiculed, he was sent back to his cell.

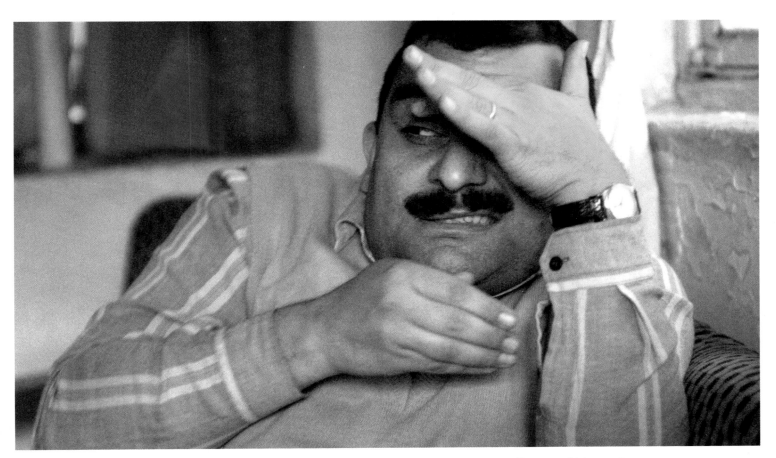

**Dhakir describes how he lifted the corner of his blindfold in an attempt to catch a glimpse of his captors.**

# Miracle of Miracles

As Dhakir awaited his unknown fate, a fellow captive who shared his cell thrashed on the hard stone floor most of the morning, screaming in pain.

"I am dying! Help me! Help me!" he yelled, desperate to escape the sharp, stabbing pain that was convulsing his abdomen. Everyone watched, helplessly.

One of the imprisoned Shiite Muslims stepped forward. "I am a leader in my Muslim Shia faith," he explained. Taking out his Koran, he began reading verses aloud and calling out the names of famous Shiite leaders who had died more than fourteen hundred years before.

The man still yelled in pain.

A Sunni Muslim then spoke up. "I think the Sunni teachings are stronger than that of Shia," he said. He opened his Koran and read some verses and called out the names of dead Sunni leaders.

No response from the man, still in agonizing pain.

Dhakir quietly asked the group if he might pray for the man. Placing his hand on the man's stomach, he prayed aloud that God would take away his pain.

After Dhakir's prayer was finished, the moans of the sick prisoner gave way to exuberant shouts: "I've been healed! I've been healed!"

Incredibly, this exact scenario repeated itself the next day, this time with a prisoner whose head was hurting. The Shiite prayed, then the Sunni. But it was only after Dhakir prayed that the man claimed he was free from pain.

God was at work in the hearts of men . . . in the bowels of Saddam's labyrinth.

After a short time, Dhakir was once again called in for interrogation. Blindfolded and hands tied—like before—he could hear the distant sounds of other prisoners being beaten as he was ushered by guards down the corridor to the interrogation room. His stomach cringed with the uncertainty of what was about to occur.

Finally brought to a stop, he stood there, waiting. Then for no reason known to him, he was told to take off the ties that bound his hands and the blindfold he was wearing. Squinting slightly after removing the mask from his eyes, Dhakir saw the faces of six men, staring at him.

"Mr. Dhakir," the lead officer intoned, "we have nothing against you, so tomorrow you will be sent home to your family."

And that was it.

Back in his cell, the other prisoners marveled that he was being sent home so quickly, after only five days. "Your Jesus is very strong," they told Dhakir. "Please pray for us. He who delivered you free will help us to be free." He assured them that he would.

Raja, Dhakir's wife, never gave up in her belief that God would bring her husband home. Tears immediately flood her eyes as she remembers the moment she saw Dhakir come through their front door.

"I could not believe my eyes," she says, smiling through her tears. The family embraced as one, praising and thanking

> After Dhakir's prayer was finished, the moans of the sick prisoner gave way to exuberant shouts: "I've been healed! I've been healed!"

God for bringing Dhakir home. "Me and my mother and sisters from the church, we also prayed and thanked God with a big hallelujah."

Even after returning home, Dhakir continued to fast and pray until the other pastors arrested with him were released—March 1, 2003.

Nineteen days later, the war began.

# Freedom Comes to Iraq

The bombs fell loudly around Baghdad's terrified residents, but for Dhakir and his family, they were the sounds of freedom on its way.

"After thirty-five years of dictatorship, enough was enough," says Dhakir.

Their home, located on the edge of Saddam's governmental palace, was too dangerous as the bombing continued night after night. The family sought shelter in a home owned by Dhakir's family in another part of the city.

"This is known as the Green Zone now, but during the bombing, this place was a hell zone," Dhakir says.

Their temporary shelter, however, did not keep them out of danger. A cluster bomb hit their home, knocking pieces of ceiling down on top of the blankets they huddled beneath, as they sang hymns and prayed. Part of a hot plastic piece from the bomb found its way to Raja's blanket but stopped there, leaving a smoldering burn on the blanket, which the family keeps as a reminder. Dhakir's car was also damaged with dents. He says he doesn't bother fixing it so he can remember each time he drives how God spared their lives.

"All of the neighbors had wounds, and their homes caught fire," recalls Raja. "But God spared us."

While hiding under their blankets each evening, they read (what else?) . . . Psalm 91, a prayer God sovereignly used to encourage both American soldiers and Iraqi citizens alike.

"We have the same Jesus," Raja says, smiling.

Shortly after the bombing campaign ended and coalition forces had invaded Baghdad, Dhakir restarted his media ministry. He currently serves as both a translator for the U.S. military as well as an Iraqi chaplain to Iraqi hospital patients.

A new, large satellite now adorns the roof of his house—a communications device forbidden under Saddam's regime, punishable by large fines and even prison time. The satellite makes it possible for Dhakir to pick up a wider variety of programs, which he continues to tape on his VCR and make copies to distribute.

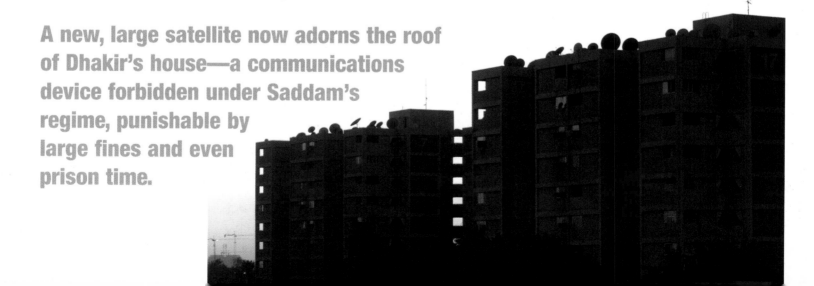

A new, large satellite now adorns the roof of Dhakir's house—a communications device forbidden under Saddam's regime, punishable by large fines and even prison time.

He has also started a new church with the help of an American army chaplain. More than 150 Iraqis, many of them new Christians, now have a place to meet and worship regularly. It's a reality that once seemed like only a dream for many of the people here.

# The Golden Period

"I want Christianity everywhere, but this is a spiritual war," says Dhakir. "Out of about twenty-five million Iraqis, we are one million Christians against twenty-four million Muslims. I don't think they will agree."

He refers to this period of time as "the golden period," a time where Iraqis are getting the opportunity to actively practice their faith. For Christians, it means underground churches are coming to the surface, Christ is being shared with neighbors, and a freedom to worship is being practiced for the first time since before the days of Saddam. But there is no guarantee it will remain this way.

More than 65 percent of the population is Shiite Muslim. A majority that could easily choose to make Iraq an Islamic state as Iraq moves toward democracy. It's a move that would force Christians to leave Iraq for good, Dhakir and Raja say. It's something the couple and others pray will never happen.

Chaplain (Colonel) Doug Carver has spent a lot of time with both Muslim and Christian leaders in Baghdad. He says his experience with Muslims has been good, and he's hopeful the country can eventually agree on freedom of religion.

"I believe the young Muslims are wanting a democracy very similar to our American life, wanting separation of church and state," he says. "The Shiites want to establish a theocracy—which could make it very difficult for Christians if it happens."

He's not sure how it will turn out.

"One of the issues is [the term] 'freedom of religion,'" Carver explains. "What does that mean? It's something we need to pray for as they try to establish a free democratic society in a Muslim part of the world."

# The Greatest Freedom

They lift their voices in joyful song and raise their hands in praise. They sing a familiar tune that many in the United States might recognize; the only difference is the Arabic words. *"King of Kings and Lord of Lords, Glory, Hallelujah."*

Their worship is expressive, earnest, and sincere. More than seventy-five families have joined the church since it began, and Dhakir and his wife make regular visits two days each week. There are Bible studies for the adults, Sunday school for the children. A light seems to shine in the eyes of everyone assembled, knowledge of Christ's love and protection.

Twenty-eight-year-old Fu'ad lived through war most of his life. He was a child during the Iraq-Iran War. As a teenager, he watched the Gulf War unfold. With the overthrow of Saddam from this most recent war, however, he is hopeful that freedom will indeed reign for the people of Iraq.

"God has opened a new door for praising Him," Fu'ad says, active in Dhakir's church and thinking about attending seminary. "It was a door that was closed to us before. He has given us the freedom to exalt His kingdom and spread His kingdom throughout Iraq. It's great."

**"God has opened a new door for praising Him. It was a door that was closed to us before. He has given us the freedom to exalt His kingdom and spread His kingdom throughout Iraq. It's great."**

**Fu'ad**

Hafa, a forty-three-year-old pharmacist, says the liberation of Iraq is "a kind of miracle."

"Jesus is everything," she says, following a church service led by Dhakir. "We were hoping something would happen the way it did in Afghanistan. I want every Iraqi to have Jesus in their heart. God made me free; to know Jesus is there, that is true freedom."

"We know that there are people praying for the 10/40 window, which is where Iraq is," says Fu'ad, who learned of this fact from the Internet. "Tell the people in the U.S. that we are thankful for them and for their prayers. We, too, are praying earnestly for the security of Iraq, for the safe and quick return of U.S. troops. And we are praying for the church—that this new seed that has sprung from this desert place will enlarge among the people, and that God will be known."

That God will be known to *all* people. Everywhere.

**" Jesus is everything. We were hoping something would happen the way it did in Afghanistan. I want every Iraqi to have Jesus in their heart. God made me free; to know Jesus is there, that is true freedom." Hafa**

**"We know that there are people praying for the 10/40 window, which is where Iraq is. Tell the people in the U.S. that we are thankful for them and for their prayers. We, too, are praying earnestly for the security of Iraq, for the safe and quick return of U.S. troops. And we are praying for the church—that this new seed that has sprung from this desert place will enlarge among the people, and that God will be known."** Fu'ad

# EPILOGUE

The story of the Iraqi War and the Iraqi people isn't over. At this writing, U.S. troops are still there. Although soldiers are returning home after a long and hard year's deployment, others have only arrived, as replacements in the rotation. Their experiences are just beginning. A blank page waits for the stories they will tell.

One thing that can be told—despite what critics say—is that the United States and coalition forces have not fought this war in vain. Their bravery and great sacrifice have allowed an oppressed people to be rescued, their land freed from a cruel dictator. By leaving behind their freedoms of comfort and security to pave the way for freedom in Iraq, these dedicated men and women have labored valiantly to ensure that our liberties back at home remain intact.

They know they're in Iraq for the right reasons. This is proven every time an Iraqi says thank-you or a child shyly waves hello or an Iraqi civilian warns them of insurgent attacks or hidden explosives. U.S. soldiers see the Iraqis as people just like them: people with hopes and dreams of a better tomorrow, yet people who also experience anger and frustration when tomorrow seems a long way off.

The Christians in the military see even more. They know the greater reason, the greater freedom for Iraqis: the freedom to worship, pray, and experience Christ for the first time. They've witnessed God's protection in ways large and small—not only for the Americans but for the Iraqis as well— and have understood God's higher reasons for keeping safe those who will glorify Him and praise His name. They per-

form their jobs with the knowledge of where they're going, beyond the battlefield. This unique peace comes only through their dependence on God, through faith in Jesus Christ.

Iraqi Christians also recognize God's grace and mercy on their country. Despite the violence, despite the death and destruction, they trust that God is leading them to a better life, a better hope for the future, for their children's future. The Iraqis, of course, rejoiced when Saddam was captured, with a fervor the Americans could only begin to understand. Dhakir's church met for their Sunday prayer service shortly after the announcement was made. In an e-mail dated December 27, 2003, he wrote:

"Catching Saddam and showing him on TV is an unexpected surprise for Iraqis . . . BECAUSE IT IS A WISE LESSON TO EVERY DICTATOR IN THE WORLD.

"The tradition here (although it is very bad) is to shoot guns in the air for celebration, but it was not very big because many said this man isn't worth spending bullets for! For comparison, the shooting in the air after the death of his sons was greater!

"Before catching Saddam, there was some amount of fear inside every Iraqi that ranged from 1 to 100 percent. Now this percentage of fear is almost near to zero. (There is some caution now for revenge from his remaining followers. We hope they will be caught also.)

"Inside my church, they feel happy, and they smile each time when I tell them to show their joy in whatever way they want, to not be afraid, because we do not have any more

Saddam agents inside churches to monitor people and write reports on their speeches or reactions or complaining."

Try as we might, we can only imagine how this must feel.

# Without Fear, without Apathy

The freedom to worship . . . without fear.

It's a freedom most Americans have taken for granted too much of the time. The liberty we enjoy each week to attend church, to raise our voices, and to raise our hands is a privilege Iraqis and others throughout the world are dying for. The military understands what this freedom means because they've seen up close those who do not have it. They've heard the stories. They've seen the underground churches now starting to surface, the pastors who once risked their lives for preaching the gospel, now openly sharing their faith in very public ways. They've watched the Iraqis embrace this new freedom like a child embracing a new teddy bear.

"God is changing the spiritual landscape of the Middle East," says Chaplain Jim Murphy, the regiment chaplain for the 82nd Airborne, 325th Regiment. "Here is where the Garden of Eden was. Here is where Nimrod's empire was. It's a spiritual gateway for hell and for the kingdom of heaven as well. What happens here affects the whole world."

The world will watch and wait.

Members of the USS *Harry S. Truman* now watch back home in the States, having returned to the shipyard in Virginia shortly after the combat phase of the war was declared over in May.

The 82nd Airborne, 325th, 3rd Battalion will also soon watch from home. They'll return to their families in North Carolina only weeks after this book goes to the printer, to reunite with spouses and hold their children—in some cases, holding children they've never seen in person.

Many of the others mentioned in these stories will also return home by early summer.

The Iraqis themselves will wait to see what will happen and how God will continue moving in their midst. Today, Dhakir and his family faithfully minister to the more than eighty-five families (450 adults and children) who have joined his church, testifying to God's protection and grace. Their media ministry is more active than ever as other churches likewise experience a surge in new growth. Their daughter, Lana, hopes to translate for the U.S. Army after she finishes college, which she attends in nearby Mosul. Their son, Basim, says he, too, wants to serve in the U.S. Army. He's developed good friendships with some of the soldiers who help guard their neighborhood.

They worry, though, about the developing constitution and whether their rights as Christians will be accounted for as the government is shaped and formed. They worry that the United States will pull out too soon, that Muslim extremists will take over the country, forming an Islamic state like its neighbor, Iran.

They pray that God will not have granted them this freedom to worship only to have it taken away.

They know, however, just as their military brothers and sisters in Christ, that no matter what happens, there is a freedom greater than the physical, greater than public worship or even private prayer. It is the freedom and the assurance of eternity with Jesus Christ. As the Bible says in 2 Corinthians 3:17: "Now the Lord is the Spirit, and where the Spirit of the Lord is, there is freedom."

Yes, indeed. A greater freedom.

# ACKNOWLEDGMENTS

This work, like so much of our lives, is really the consequence of what others do to make it feasible. Betsy, my wife and helpmate for more than three decades, has a faith and understanding that makes it possible for me to hang around with heroes like those in this book. Her prayers and those of our children and their mates sustain me on long trips to cover the brave young Americans who guard us in faraway, dangerous places. The soldiers, sailors, airmen, and Marines who contributed to this work deserve most of the credit. But they are not alone.

In two trips to Iraq and the Persian Gulf, Sara Horn has demonstrated a talent for words that I can only envy. Jim Veneman, who accompanied Sara on those missions, has shown such skill with a camera that I wonder why I ever bother to take a picture. Diana Lawrence has a gift for construction and an eye for design that is unparalleled. And no one can lay claim to working better under pressure than Lawrence Kimbrough, who did the text styling for this beautiful work, or B&H Senior Editor Gary Terashita.

All of them made this beautiful testament to faith and freedom possible.

*—Oliver L. North*


Perhaps one of the least reported stories of the Iraq War is the faith of the U.S. soldier. While we've seen stories and photos of baptisms, chaplain ministries, and minority religions, these have only touched the surface. The deeper question of why these soldiers believe in God and the results of that belief can still be explored. That's why I'm incredibly grateful as a Christian and a journalist for this project and the opportunity for a small part in telling and sharing with others these stories of Christians in the military.

I am especially thankful to God for His providence and protection that we've seen throughout these assignments and the completion of this book. I am also very grateful to my husband Cliff for his amazing support and willingness to care for our little boy while his wife travels to war zones halfway across the world! Thank you for understanding and sharing my passion. I love you so much.

Jim Veneman is such a talented photojournalist who has been as much a mentor and teacher to me as a friend. Thank you for sharing in these travels with me and for having a mutual excitement and enthusiasm for reporting the story. I have learned so much from you over the years, and I thank God for you and your family.

Thanks to Oliver North for helping make the completion of this book a reality. It was an honor to meet you. Also, I must say a special thanks to SFC Michael Yarber and the 372nd Mobile Public Affairs Detachment for helping us get to Baghdad and for your hospitality. You made a huge difference in the outcome of this book.

A big thanks goes to all of the wonderful people at Broadman & Holman: Gary Terashita, Lawrence Kimbrough, David Shepherd, and especially Diana Lawrence for her amazing design work and ability to understand and communicate the message visually. Outstanding! It has been a joy to work with each of you.

I would be remiss if I didn't thank Will Hall and Baptist Press. Who would have thought that one conversation about a story idea would lead to all this? Thanks for your shared commitment in reporting what God is doing in the hearts and lives of people.

I greatly appreciate Mike Arrington, Rob Phillips, and my colleagues in the office of corporate communications at LifeWay Christian Resources. Thank you for your support and encouragement. All of you continue to teach me new things every day for which I am grateful to learn!

Finally, I must thank the brave men and women of our U.S. forces we had the privilege of meeting aboard the USS *Truman* and in Baghdad. Commander Chaplain Dunn, Chaplain (Capt.) Eddie Cook, and all of the others—your commitment to God and to your country is inspiring and humbling, and I thank God for all of you. I pray that this book finds you home with your own families and the knowledge that you've served your best for both your country and your Creator. God bless you.

*—Sara Horn*

# THE STORY BEHIND THE STORIES

Jim Veneman and I made two trips to the Middle East in 2003, and each experience had its own unique and memorable moments. People are always asking us about the stories that didn't show up in print. Here are a few snippets from behind the text and photographs. We hope you enjoy reading them as much as we did remembering.

## The *Truman*

When we got the word our trip was a "go"—a day earlier than expected—we only had six hours to pack and get to the airport before our flight left. As I waited for Jim, who was coming from his home three hours away, I also waited for my passport (which hadn't yet arrived). As I whispered a desperate prayer to God, my cell phone rang. It was the airport post office saying they had my passport. Two minutes later, it was in my hand, and we made it on the flight . . . just in time.

We spent the first week of the war on the *Truman*, working twenty-hour days, sleeping and taking catnaps as we could. As we witnessed the first planes launching during "shock and awe," a flash went off from where the media had assembled on an observation deck. We had been warned about flash photography, which can pose dangers to aviators and airmen. The Navy officers in charge were about to throw all of us off the deck until they discovered it had been an excited sailor—not a photographer—who had made the treacherous mistake.

We slept in the men and women's supply berthing areas, right underneath the flight deck. My rack, the top of three stacked beds in a room that held three hundred, shook every time a plane launched or landed.

It was hard leaving the ship the day of our departure. As we walked through the mess deck, we ran into many of the friends we had made along the way. They wouldn't be coming with us. One young man we met right before we walked onto the flight deck to board our plane told us he, too, was from Nashville. Knowing we were returning there, he said, "Kiss the grass for me."

## Baghdad

Where the *Truman* trip had taken only two weeks to put together, the trip to Baghdad was two and a half months in the making. Initially, we had gone through the Air Force to get permission to embed with a unit whose chaplain I had been in contact with at BIAP. We did everything they asked—getting the right shots, filling out the right paperwork, even taking a short antiterrorism course on CD-ROM. Still no word when we might leave.

By mid-November, we were beginning to doubt the trip would happen at all. Then a phone call came from Oliver North: "Get on a plane for Kuwait." We'd been in contact with SFC Michael Yarber, a reservist with a public affairs unit in Baghdad, who we were planning on staying with once we got there. We left two days after North's phone call.

When we got to Kuwait, we discovered we were still missing country clearance. For two days, we waited for something to happen. At breakfast that Tuesday morning, we talked about faith and trust. We firmly believed God was in this trip and behind this book, that He would provide what we needed. When I got back to my room, I had an e-mail from Yarber. He had the country clearance codes in hand, and we were on our way.

There were a few tense moments while we were there. As we rode through the Green Zone with Yarber one afternoon, an older woman wearing a traditional Muslim covering from head to toe approached the Humvee. Yarber pushed the accelerator to the floor, and as we left the woman behind, he muttered something about that situation having "bad all over it." Jim also remembers nearly falling out of a truck one day when our driver switched lanes under an overpass. The driver explained he was avoiding any bombs or grenades someone might toss from the bridge above.

On Saturday afternoon we had planned to cover the removal of several Saddam heads that were still atop the governmental palace, but the work was canceled due to some of the workers' receiving death threats. That left us with no story to cover and what we felt was a lot of wasted time. We thought it would be interesting to talk with an Iraqi family, so we began looking for Dhakir, the Iraqi translator we had met at the hospital. We went several different places trying to find him, with no success. As we parked and got ready to walk back into the house where we were staying, I stood at the corner, praying that God would provide the story we should cover. Just then, an Iraqi car turned the corner. It was Dhakir. He stopped, and we quickly jumped in his car for a visit with him and his family in their home in downtown Baghdad. Later he told us that he never drove that way normally. When we told him we'd been looking for him, his reply was, "God kicked me to you."

God gave us confirmation time and time again that He wanted this book to be written in His way and His timing. Just as the military have seen it firsthand, we also saw God at work. His way is best. All He asks us to do is listen and obey.